The Structural Design Toolkit for C#

Composition, Delegation, and Collaboration through Six Core Design Patterns

Vaskaran Sarcar

Apress®

The Structural Design Toolkit for C#: Composition, Delegation, and Collaboration through Six Core Design Patterns

Vaskaran Sarcar
Near Garia Station, Post: Garia
Kuntala Furniture, 2nd Floor
Kolkata, West Bengal, India

ISBN-13 (pbk): 979-8-8688-3028-0 ISBN-13 (electronic): 979-8-8688-3029-7
https://doi.org/10.1007/979-8-8688-3029-7

Managing Director, Apress Media LLC: Welmoed Spahr
Acquisitions Editor: Smriti Srivastava
Editorial Assistant: Marina Engler

Cover designed by eStudioCalamar

Cover image designed by Freepik (www.freepik.com)

Distributed to the book trade worldwide by Springer Science+Business Media New York, 1 New York Plaza, New York, NY 10004. Phone 1-800-SPRINGER, fax (201) 348-4505, e-mail orders-ny@springer-sbm.com, or visit www.springeronline.com. Apress Media, LLC is a Delaware LLC and the sole member (owner) is Springer Science + Business Media Finance Inc (SSBM Finance Inc). SSBM Finance Inc is a **Delaware** corporation.

For information on translations, please e-mail booktranslations@springernature.com; for reprint, paperback, or audio rights, please e-mail bookpermissions@springernature.com.

Apress titles may be purchased in bulk for academic, corporate, or promotional use. eBook versions and licenses are also available for most titles. For more information, reference our Print and eBook Bulk Sales web page at http://www.apress.com/bulk-sales.

Any source code or other supplementary material referenced by the author in this book is available to readers on GitHub (https://github.com/Apress/The-Structural-Design-Toolkit-for-C-). For more detailed information, please visit https://www.apress.com/gp/services/source-code.

If disposing of this product, please recycle the paper

Dedicated to the Gang of Four and the pioneers of object-oriented design, whose timeless ideas continue to inspire flexible, maintainable, and scalable software systems.

Table of Contents

About the Author

Vaskaran Sarcar brings a unique blend of academic rigor and industry leadership to his technical writing. A National GATE Scholar, Vaskaran has leveraged over 18 years of professional experience in teaching, software development, and programming to become an established author. He is the author of 20 technical books published by Apress, including multiple editions of well-received titles such as *Java Design Patterns* and *Design Patterns in C#*, with his book *Interactive C#* also translated into Japanese.

Before focusing on full-time authorship, he spent a decade at HP India's PPS R&D Hub, **serving as a Senior Software Engineer and later as a Team Lead**, where he specialized in designing automation test frameworks and resolving critical defects. Vaskaran is passionate about transforming complex ideas into accessible knowledge for learners worldwide. You can connect with him on LinkedIn at https://www.linkedin.com/in/vaskaransarcar/ and explore his books from the following links:

Springer Catalog: https://link.springer.com/search?facet-content-type=%22Book%22&query=vaskaran+sarcar&sortOrder=newestFirst

Amazon Author Page: https://www.amazon.com/author/vaskaran_sarcar

About the Technical Reviewer

Shekhar Kumar Maravi is a software architect specializing in design and development whose main interests are programming languages, Linux system programming, the Linux kernel, algorithms, and data structures. He obtained his master's degree in Computer Science and Engineering from the Indian Institute of Technology Bombay. After graduation, he joined Hewlett-Packard's R&D Hub in India to work on Printer Firmware. Currently, he is a Product & Solution Development Team Lead for automated pathology lab diagnostic devices at Siemens Healthcare R&D division. He can be reached via LinkedIn at https://www.linkedin.com/in/shekharmaravi.

Acknowledgments

At first, I thank the Almighty. I believe that I was able to complete this book with His blessings. I extend my deepest gratitude and thanks to:

Shekhar Kumar Maravi—the technical reviewer for this book and many of my earlier works. Your unwavering support has been invaluable.

Smriti, Marina, and the Apress team—I sincerely thank each of you for giving me another opportunity to work with you.

Abirami, the copy editor (Jade Tumale), and the Production team members (Jagathesan, Selvakumar and Vinoth)—thanks to each of you for your exceptional support in beautifying my work. Your efforts are extraordinary.

Finally, I thank the people in various online communities, particularly the C# developer community, the .NET developer community, and the Stack Overflow community, who share their knowledge in various ways. In fact, I thank everyone who contributed, directly or indirectly, to this work.

Introduction

Design pattern concepts are universal, and applying them effectively in C# opens opportunities to build flexible, maintainable, and reusable software.

Design patterns gained prominence through the Gang of Four's (GoF) classic book, *Design Patterns: Elements of Reusable Object-Oriented Software* (Addison-Wesley, 1994). That seminal work, written with C++ in mind, predates C# itself. C# 1.0 was released in January 2002. Since then, it has steadily evolved and matured, gaining many powerful language and library features. This naturally raises an important question: **Do we still need design patterns in modern C#?**

The answer is yes. Many design patterns form the foundation of today's programming practices. They do not rely on unusual language features or clever tricks; rather, they capture proven approaches to structuring object-oriented systems. When direct language support is unavailable, patterns often require additional effort—but that effort pays off in long-term flexibility, clarity, and reuse. It is, therefore, no surprise that the GoF book remains widely read and influential even today.

The classical GoF book cataloged 23 patterns into three categories: creational, structural, and behavioral. Some patterns have become less central over time because modern languages and frameworks provide built-in support for their underlying ideas. In fact, the GoF authors later revisited their original catalog. They discussed how certain patterns could be reconsidered, reclassified, or deemphasized (see the interview at https://www.informit.com/articles/article.aspx?p=1404056&lang=en with Erich Gamma, Richard Helm, and Ralph Johnson). **However, several patterns remain essential and highly relevant in 2026. This book discusses six such essential patterns, supported by multiple examples and case studies.**

How Is the Book Organized?

At a high level, the book is divided into two parts—**Part I** and **Part II**. The first six chapters belong to **Part I**, whereas the final chapter belongs to **Part II**. To give you an idea, let me summarize the contents of **Part I**:

Chapter 1 explains the usefulness of composition over inheritance and discusses the Decorator pattern, providing two sample implementations.

Chapter 2 demonstrates how to integrate third-party code using the **Adapter** pattern, allowing incompatible classes to work together. This chapter illustrates both the object adapter and the class adapter and explains how a class adapter can play the role of a two-way adapter.

Chapter 3 includes two different implementations to explain the **Proxy** pattern, including a demonstration of how a proxy-based solution can be **combined with the Decorator pattern**.

Chapter 4 demystifies the Facade pattern with two different implementations. The first example **simplifies the use of an internal subsystem**, and the follow-up example discusses how this pattern can provide a **unified interface over heterogeneous external APIs** with different rules and method signatures.

Chapter 5 explains how to decouple an abstraction from its implementation using the Bridge pattern with two different examples. The first example shows how composition can enable flexible combinations of items and pricing strategies at runtime. The follow-up example extends this idea further by focusing on a *Refined Abstraction*, showing that specialized behavior can be added to a specific abstraction without modifying the base class or the implementation hierarchy.

Chapter 6 discusses the **Composite** pattern with multiple examples, including examples of composite structures available in C# libraries.

Part II combines all the knowledge that you learned in the first six chapters into a single project. This hands-on workshop is designed to show you how multiple structural design patterns collaborate within a single system to solve real-world design challenges.

Appendix A suggests additional resources for further reading.

Appendix B lists my other books for your reference.

You can enjoy learning by analyzing these implementations and asking questions about any doubts. Throughout this book, you will see many "Q&A Sessions." Each question in these Q&A sessions is marked with **Q<Chapter_no>.<Question_no>**. For example, **Q3.2** means question number 2 of Chapter 3. These are presented to make your future learning easier and enjoyable, but most importantly, they make you confident as a developer.

You can download the entire book's source code from the publisher's website: https://github.com/Apress/The-Structural-Design-Toolkit-for-C-

Prerequisite Knowledge

I expect you to be familiar with C# and how to compile or run a C# application. In short, the target readers of this book are those who have an understanding of pure object-oriented concepts, such as polymorphism, inheritance, abstraction, and encapsulation. While implementing the patterns, I want you to make the most out of C# by harnessing the power of both object-oriented programming (OOP) and functional programming (FP).

Who Is This Book For?

You can read this book if the answer is "yes" to the following questions:

- Are you familiar with C# and basic object-oriented concepts such as polymorphism, inheritance, abstraction, and encapsulation?
- Do you know how to set up your coding environment?
- Do you want to explore the listed design patterns in C# step by step?

You may want to skip this book if the answer is "yes" to any of the following:

- Are you uncomfortable working with examples developed using Microsoft Visual Studio IDE on a Windows environment?
- Are you already confident with GoF design patterns and looking for advanced or lesser-known patterns beyond those covered here?

Guidelines for Using This Book

Here are some suggestions so that you can get the most out of this book:

Sequential reading of these chapters can help you learn faster. This is because some useful and related topics may have already been discussed in a previous chapter, and I have not repeated those discussions in the later chapters.

The programs in this book should give you the expected output in the upcoming versions of C# as well. Though I believe that these results should not vary in other environments, you know that software systems can sometimes behave differently across environments and versions. So, I recommend that if you want to see the same output, it will be better if you can mimic the same environment.

Useful Software

During the development of this book, software updates kept coming, and I also kept updating my tools accordingly. By the time the draft was completed, the development environment was running on **C#14.0 targeting .NET 10** with **Visual Studio 2026 Community Edition (Insiders [11811.120])**.

The good news for you is that this community edition is free of cost. If you do not use the Windows operating system, you can also use Visual Studio Code, a source-code editor developed by Microsoft that runs on Windows, macOS, and Linux operating systems. This multi-platform code editor is also free. However, I recommend that you check the license and privacy statement as well. This is because this statement may change in the future.

The examples in this book deliberately focus on the **fundamental object-oriented constructs of C#**, rather than on version-specific or preview features. As a result, the code is not tied to a particular C# release and should execute smoothly on current and upcoming versions of C# and Visual Studio.

You can download Visual Studio 2026 from the official link (https://visualstudio.microsoft.com/downloads/) and expect to see the screenshot shown in Figure 1.

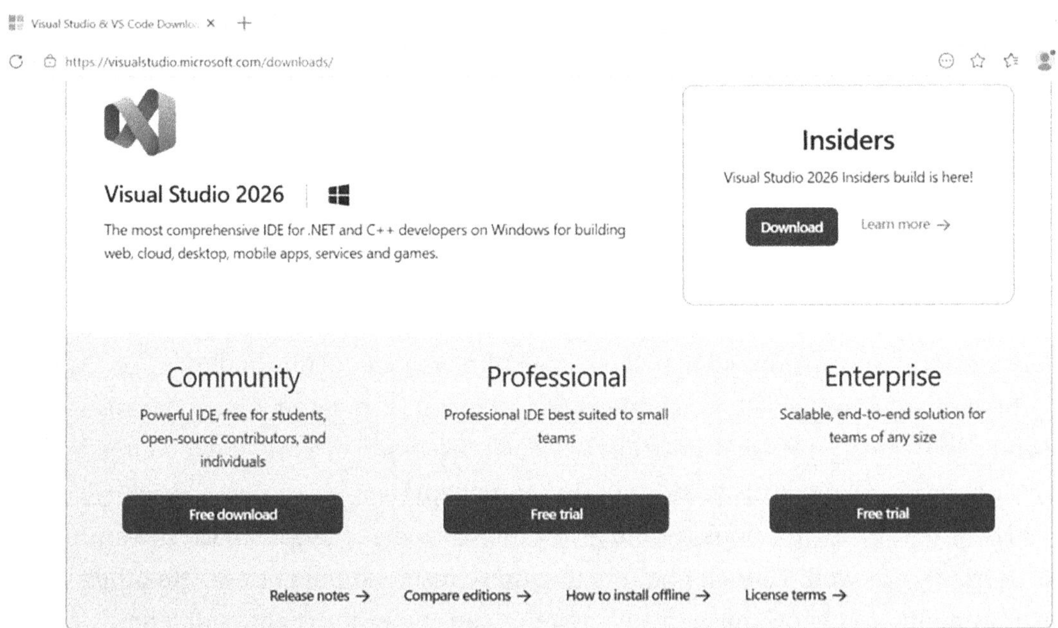

***Figure 1.** The official download link for Visual Studio 2026*

Note The Visual Studio Code is also available at the same link. At the time of this writing, this link works fine, and the information is correct. However, the link and policies may change in the future. The same comment applies to all the mentioned links in this book.

Before coding, I often use a pen or a pencil, markers, and a whiteboard to draft ideas. For the Class diagrams in this book, however, I used Visual Studio's Class Designer[1] tool to generate class diagrams. These diagrams help you visualize and communicate the designs. Class Designer allows classes and their relationships to be modeled directly from code. You can learn more about it from the official link supplied as a footnote on this page.

Conventions Used in This Book

This book uses modern C# project settings where **implicit usings** are enabled. As a result, some commonly used namespaces (such as System and System.Collections.Generic) may not always appear explicitly in the code samples. **These namespaces are automatically available through global using directives generated by the compiler**. For clarity, important using statements are occasionally shown, especially in the early chapters.

To keep the examples organized, each demonstration in this book is placed in its respective namespace. Any common code used across multiple demonstrations is placed in a separate namespace. For example, since Chapter 2 discusses the Adapter pattern, you'll find all code for this chapter in **Ch02.Adapter**. There are two main demonstrations in this chapter. The code specific to each demonstration is placed inside **Ch02.Adapter.Demo1** and **Ch02.Adapter.Demo2** namespaces. The common code that is used by these demonstrations can be found in **Ch02.Adapter.Common**.

Due to page width limitations, some long lines of code—particularly string literals—may appear split across multiple lines in the printed layout. **Unless otherwise indicated, such lines should be read as a single continuous statement.**

[1] https://learn.microsoft.com/en-us/visualstudio/ide/class-designer/designing-and-viewing-classes-and-types?view=visualstudio

Finally, all the programs, their corresponding outputs, and the book's important notes use the same font and structure. To draw your attention, I have made some places bold. For example, consider the following code fragment (taken from Chapter 5, where I discussed the changes in Demonstration 2) as follows:

```
// The using statements and namespace details are not shown here for brevity
public class Mobile(IPricingScheme scheme, double printedPrice)
 : ElectronicItem(scheme)
{
  private readonly double _printedPrice = printedPrice;
  protected override double GetPrintedPrice()
  {
     return _printedPrice;
  }
  #region This specific method is added for Demonstration 2
  // This method is added to provide a special promotional discount
  public double GetFestiveTimePrice(double discountPercent)
  {
   double priceBeforeDiscount = GetFinalPrice();
   return priceBeforeDiscount * (1 - discountPercent / 100);
  }
  #endregion
}
```

You may also notice that some code lines may appear visually wrapped due to the width of the printed page or your device's screen.

Errata

I have tried my level best to ensure the accuracy of the content. However, mistakes can happen. I maintain an "Errata" page and, if necessary, will provide updates or announcements there. So, I suggest that you visit those pages to receive any important corrections or updates.

Final Words

This is a useful topic that can assist you throughout your career. As you learn and review these concepts, I suggest you write your code; only then will you master this area. There is no shortcut for this. Do you know the ancient story of Euclid and Ptolemy, the ruler of Egypt? Euclid's approach to mathematics was based on logical reasoning and rigorous proofs, and Ptolemy asked Euclid if there was an easier way to learn mathematics. Euclid's reply to the ruler? "**There is no royal road to geometry.**" Though you are not studying geometry, the essence of this reply applies here. You must study these concepts and code. Do not give up when you face challenges. They are the indicators that you are growing better.

C# is a great language. Using it to implement essential design patterns is a great idea. Let's get started!

PART I

Patterns for Scalable C# Architecture

Flexible architecture allows you to add functionality to objects without modifying their original source code—an essential capability for ensuring a project scales effectively rather than becoming difficult to maintain.

In this first part of the book, you will explore **six core structural design patterns**. These patterns demonstrate how to organize classes and objects into larger, more efficient structures. You'll use

- **The Decorator (Chapter 1)** pattern to add responsibilities dynamically
- **The Adapter (Chapter 2)** pattern to convert incompatible interfaces
- **The Proxy (Chapter 3)** pattern to control access and performance
- **The Facade (Chapter 4)** pattern to provide a simplified entry point
- **The Bridge (Chapter 5)** pattern to separate abstraction from implementation
- **The Composite (Chapter 6)** pattern to model part-whole relationships and handle hierarchies

Once you master these patterns, you will have the architectural foundation needed to build scalable and maintainable systems in C#. This is why these structural patterns serve as the foundation for **Part II** of this book.

CHAPTER 1

Decorator Pattern

Composition is a widely used alternative to inheritance in programming and often provides a better design payoff. This chapter discusses the Decorator pattern that relies on object composition. This pattern is also known as the **Wrapper pattern.**

Concept

The Gang of Four (GoF) defined the intent of the Decorator pattern as follows:

> Attach additional responsibilities to an object dynamically. Decorators provide a flexible alternative to subclassing for extending functionality.

Now the question is **what is a decorator (or a wrapper)? You can think of it as a topping that surrounds the main dish to enhance the taste without changing its core. Similarly, in programming, you can surround an object to add functionality using an enclosing object—often referred to as a wrapper—which conforms to the interface of the component it decorates.** This is a powerful technique because you can add or remove a wrapper as needed without compromising the functionality of the original object.

Consider a scenario that is very common in the software industry: you need to work on a piece of code that was written by someone else. Typically, while enhancing a feature to attract new customers, you cannot alter the existing workflow. Why? The software must continue to support existing customers. It is also possible that you were not part of the team that wrote the first version of the software, so you do not have complete control from the beginning. Wrappers are useful in such situations. As previously stated, in this case, you can add new functionality on top of the existing functionality to support new customers. In fact, by using different types of wrappers, you can support different types of customers.

V. Sarcar, *The Structural Design Toolkit for C#*, https://doi.org/10.1007/979-8-8688-3029-7_1

It is interesting to note that since decorators (a.k.a. wrappers) are often added dynamically, it is perfectly fine if you do not want them in a later phase of development, because the original object can still work independently. The upcoming example will make the concept clearer to you.

Real-Life Example

Consider a group of customers who would like to have their dream homes. However, we all know that the budget and mindset of every individual are different—one customer can be happy to own a home with some basic facilities, whereas another customer may prefer to have some luxuries, such as a personal gym or a swimming pool (or both). It is also possible that a customer who opts for a home with some basic facilities today can upgrade their home tomorrow by adding a gym or a swimming pool. Each of these luxuries (a gym or a swimming pool) acts as a decorator in this example.

Computer World Example

The I/O stream implementations in the .NET Framework, .NET Core, and Java use the Decorator pattern. For example:

- In C#, the `BufferedStream` class wraps another `Stream` object to provide buffering functionality (this is discussed in detail in Q1.8).
- In Java, the `java.io.BufferedOutputStream` class can decorate any `java.io.OutputStream` object as well.

Implementation

Let's write a program to mimic the real-life example that I just described. Just like a mathematical problem can be solved in different ways, an implementation can be made following different approaches. To fulfill the requirement, typically, you may like to use plain inheritance (subclassing). However, that decision can cause problems later. Let's understand it.

Problem of Subclassing

Assume that you try to fulfill the requirement using multilevel inheritance as follows:

```
class Home
{
   // Some code, if any
}

#region Problem-1
class Gym : Home
{
   // Some code, if any
}
class SwimmingPool : Gym
{
   // Some code, if any
}
#endregion
```

This isn't a good approach because to get a swimming pool, you're forced to get a gym, which a customer may not want. By similar logic, the following structure is not a good choice either (because to get a gym, you are **forced to get** a swimming pool that a customer may not want):

```
// There is no change in the Home class.
// It is not repeated for brevity.
class SwimmingPool : Home
{
   // Some code, if any
}
class Gym : SwimmingPool
{
   // Some code, if any
}
```

You can see that **subclassing in this case makes the design impractical.**

Now, let's assume that you start with a hierarchical inheritance where the Gym and SwimmingPool classes both inherit from the Home class, as shown in Figure 1-1.

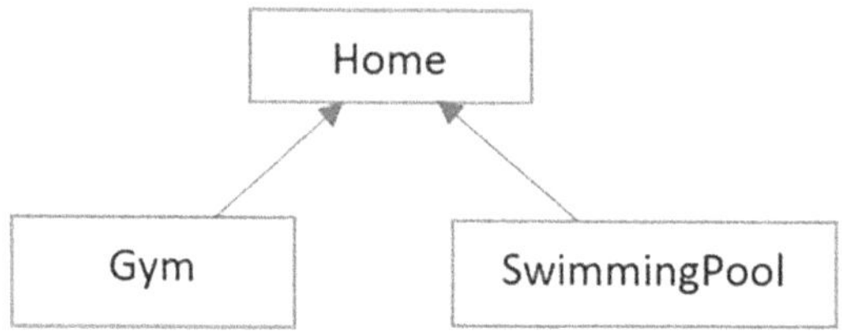

***Figure 1-1.** Both the Gym and SwimmingPool classes inherit from the Home class*

Now, to get a home with a swimming pool and a gym, you end up with the design as shown in Figure 1-2.

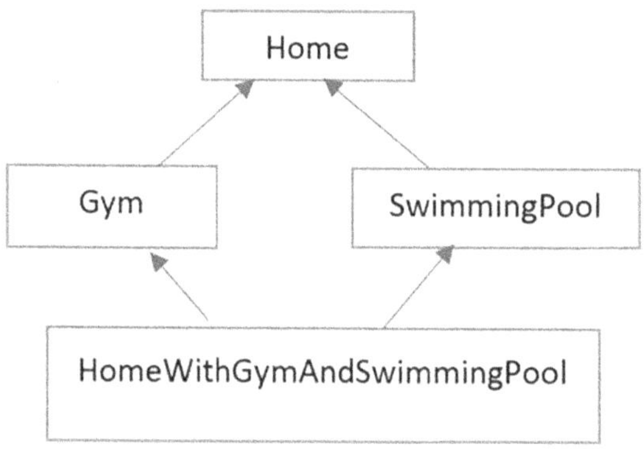

***Figure 1-2.** The HomeWithGymAndSwimmingPool class needs to inherit from multiple base classes*

However, you cannot have multiple base classes in C#. So, any construct like the following will result in a compilation error:

```
// There is no change in the Home class.
 // It is not repeated for brevity.
  class Gym : Home
  {
     // Some code, if any
  }
  class SwimmingPool : Home
  {
     // Some code, if any
  }
```

```
class HomeWithGymAndSwimmingPool : Gym, SwimmingPool  // Error
{
   // Some code
}
```

Once again, the plain subclassing technique does not provide the ideal solution! You might not be fully convinced yet! After recognizing the problem, let's assume that you opt for the following interface:

```
interface ILuxury
{
   void AddGym();
   void AddSwimmingPool();
}
```

Now you can have a class that can implement this interface. For example, here is an AdvancedHome class that extends the Home class and implements the ILuxury interface:

```
class AdvancedHome : Home, ILuxury // OK
{
   public void AddGym()
   {
      // Some code, if any
   }

   public void AddSwimmingPool()
   {
      // Some code, if any
   }
}
```

But again, this approach is rigid. If a customer opts for a home with only one of these luxuries, the class is still forced to implement both methods. You can try to bypass this by throwing an exception for the unwanted feature as follows:

```
public void AddGym()
{
   // Some code, if any
   throw new NotImplementedException();
}
```

Note The NotImplementedException inherits from SystemException, and it is available in the System namespace.

This is often used as a placeholder during development, but in this context, it violates proper interface design because the class cannot meaningfully support all interface methods. Introducing this kind of code is also risky because it can break a working solution. How? You need to understand the Liskov Substitution Principle (LSP) in this context. Since it is another big topic, it is beyond the scope of this chapter.

Author's Note: A detailed discussion with examples on LSP is included in my other book, *Simple and Efficient Programming with C#, Second Edition.*[1] If interested, you can also refer to the online explanation of the Liskov Substitution Principle.[2]

To avoid this, you may follow the Interface Segregation Principle (ISP) and segregate the ILuxury interface. Yes, this time it can work! But in this chapter, we'll search for an alternative approach.

POINTS TO REMEMBER

Subclassing may be impractical (or impossible) in certain scenarios. Even if it is possible, you may end up with too many subclasses to support every possible combination (i.e., it causes the explosion of subclasses). Maintaining a large number of subclasses is an additional overhead. The Decorator pattern can help you overcome those difficulties.

Using Object Composition

Let us see how a wrapper can help. **Using a wrapper, you surround an object with another object.** It forwards requests to the original component and can perform additional operations before or after those requests. **You can add an unlimited number of responsibilities using this concept.** The following figures help you understand this. Let's see them:

[1] https://link.springer.com/book/10.1007/978-1-4842-8737-8

[2] https://en.wikipedia.org/wiki/Liskov_substitution_principle

Figure 1-3 shows that a gym surrounds a home.

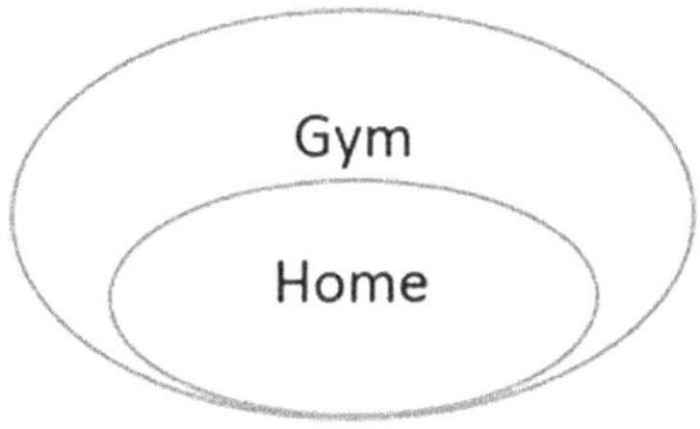

Figure 1-3. *A gym surrounds a home*

Figure 1-4 shows that a swimming pool surrounds a home.

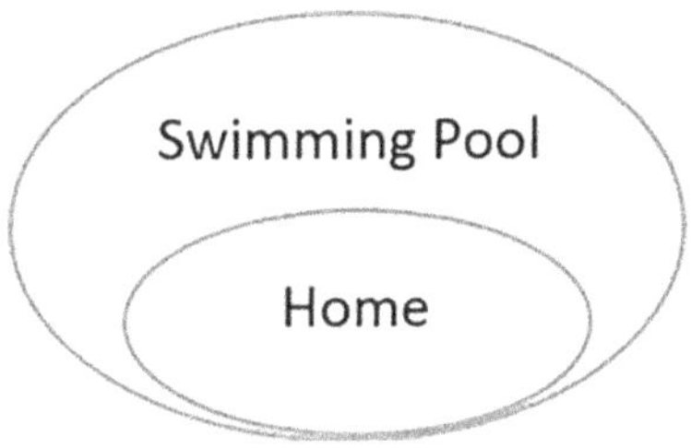

Figure 1-4. *A swimming pool surrounds a home*

Figure 1-5 shows that a gym first surrounds a home, and then the structure is further surrounded by a swimming pool.

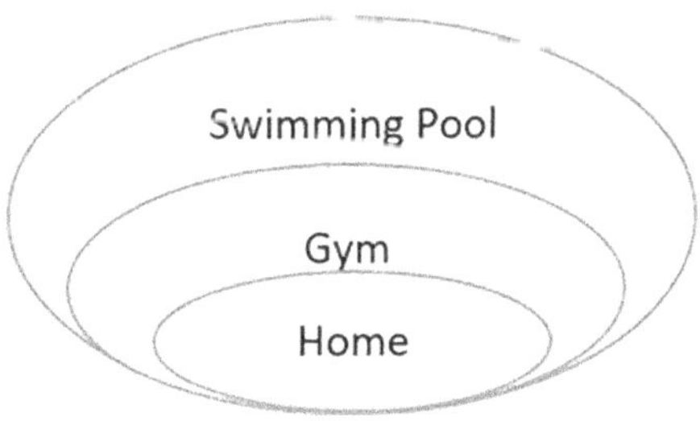

Figure 1-5. *A gym and a swimming pool surround a home*

Figure 1-6 shows that a home is surrounded by a swimming pool and a gym again. However, this time, the order is reversed—you first surround the home with a swimming pool, and then you surround the structure with a gym.

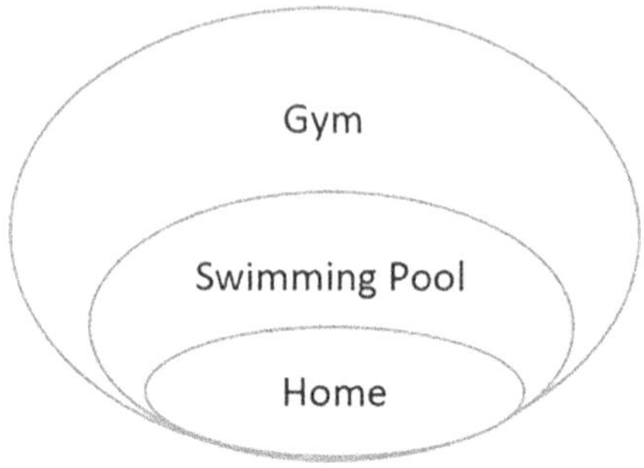

Figure 1-6. *First, a swimming pool surrounds a home. Then, a gym surrounds this structure again*

Note Following the same technique, you can add multiple gyms, swimming pools, or any other luxury elements dynamically, without altering the base object.

Let us now implement the idea. In this demonstration, five key players are involved: **Home**, **BasicHome**, **Luxury**, **Gym**, and **SwimmingPool**.

REMINDER

As discussed in the coding conventions used in this book, all code in this chapter is placed in Ch01.Decorator. The specific codes for Demonstration 1 and Demonstration 2 are placed inside the subfolders Demo1 and Demo2, respectively.

- The first two form an inheritance hierarchy and are placed inside the folder **Home**.
- The last three form another hierarchy and are placed inside the **Facilities** folder.

Author's Note: This second hierarchy is designed to add facilities (in programming terms—functionalities).

The IHome interface is defined as follows:

```
namespace Ch01.Decorator.Home
{
   public interface IHome
   {
      void Create();
   }
}
```

The BasicHome class implements the IHome interface and is defined as follows:

```
using static System.Console;

namespace Ch01.Decorator.Home
{
   public class BasicHome : IHome
   {
      public void Create()
      {
         WriteLine("A home with some basic facilities is made.");
      }
   }
}
```

Now let's look at the contents of the Facilities folder, beginning with the Luxury class. Before you see this class, I'd like you to remember the following points:

- In C#, you can have an abstract class without any abstract methods in it, but the reverse is not true, that is, if a class contains an abstract method, it means that the class itself is incomplete and you are forced to mark it with the abstract keyword. Here, Luxury is an abstract class, even though it does not contain any abstract methods. Therefore, you cannot instantiate it directly.
- Also, when you instantiate a concrete subclass of Luxury, you must pass an IHome object to which the luxuries are applied.

- From C#12 onward, the use of primary constructors is common. The following code segment shows its usage:

```
using Ch01.Decorator.Home;

// Luxury.cs

namespace Ch01.Decorator.Facilities
{
    public abstract class Luxury(IHome home) : IHome
    {
        protected readonly IHome _home = home;

        public virtual void Create()
        {
            _home.Create();
        }
    }
}
```

Here is an alternative version of the Luxury class that does not use the primary constructor:

```
// There is no change in the namespace declaration

#region Alternative code without primary constructor

public abstract class Luxury : IHome
{
    protected IHome _home;
    public Luxury(IHome home)
    {
     this._home = home;
    }
    public virtual void Create()
    {
      _home.Create();
    }
 }
#endregion
```

POINT TO NOTE

Though the Microsoft Visual Studio IDE recommends the use of primary constructors, the choice is up to you. However, I have used **primary constructors sparingly** in this book, only where they simplify the code without affecting the understanding of the design pattern. In cases where constructor logic is important to the discussion, I have used the **traditional constructor syntax** for clarity. You can learn about the primary constructors from the official link https://learn.microsoft.com/en-us/dotnet/csharp/whats-new/tutorials/primary-constructors

The Gym class inherits from the Luxury class and overrides the Create method as follows:

// Gym.cs

```
using Ch01.Decorator.Home;
using static System.Console;

namespace Ch01.Decorator.Facilities
{
   public class Gym(IHome home) : Luxury(home)
   {
      public override void Create()
      {
         base.Create();
         WriteLine("A gym is ready.");
      }
   }
}
```

Although the SwimmingPool class is very similar to the Gym class, let's review it as well so that you can easily match the output in Demonstration 1:

// SwimmingPool.cs

```
using Ch01.Decorator.Home;
using static System.Console;
```

```
namespace Ch01.Decorator.Facilities
{
    public class SwimmingPool(IHome home) : Luxury(home)
    {
        public override void Create()
        {
            base.Create();
            WriteLine("One swimming pool is made.");
        }
    }
}
```

POINT TO NOTE

Gym and SwimmingPool classes extend the Luxury class and override its Create() method. Each subclass first delegates the call to the wrapped IHome object by invoking base.Create() and then adds its own specific feature (a print message in this example). This demonstrates how decorators can attach additional responsibilities to an object at runtime without modifying its structure.

Class Diagram

Figure 1-7 shows the relationships between the discussed classes.

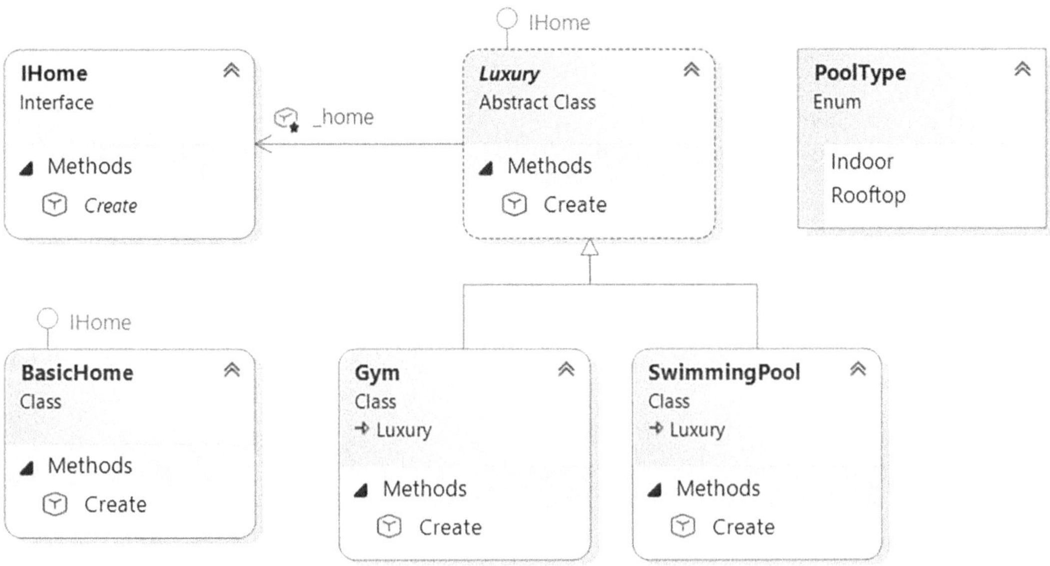

***Figure 1-7.** The class diagram shows the relationships among the key participants in Demonstration 1*

Demonstration 1

Let's exercise the complete code using the following demonstration:

```
using Ch01.Decorator.Home;
using Ch01.Decorator.Facilities;
using static System.Console;

namespace Ch01.Decorator.Demo1
{
   public class DecoratorDemo1
   {
      public static void Main()
      {
         IHome home = new BasicHome();
         home.Create();
         WriteLine("=========");
```

```
            // Adding a gym
            home = new Gym(home);
            home.Create();
            WriteLine("=========");

            // Adding a swimming pool
            home = new SwimmingPool(home);
            home.Create();
            WriteLine("=========");
        }
    }
}
```

Output

Here is the expected output:

```
A home with some basic facilities is made.
=========
A home with some basic facilities is made.
A gym is ready.
=========
A home with some basic facilities is made.
A gym is ready.
One swimming pool is made.
=========
```

Top-level Statements

Since C#9, you can use top-level statements. Using those, Demonstration 1 can be shortened as

```
// There is no change in the using statements. Those are not shown
// to avoid repetition.

#region Using top-level statements

IHome home = new BasicHome();
home.Create();
WriteLine("=========");
```

```
// Adding a gym
home = new Gym(home);
home.Create();
WriteLine("=========");

// Adding a swimming pool
home = new SwimmingPool(home);
home.Create();
WriteLine("=========");
#endregion
```

Interestingly, I did not use this approach in this book. **It is because a project can contain only one source file with top-level statements.** However, while organizing codes for this book, I have placed multiple demonstrations (in a particular chapter) inside the same project. With this setting, you can change the startup object before running the intended demonstration. If you do not know the steps, do not worry! I'll show you the steps as we discuss the execution of Demonstration 2, which is coming next.

Demonstration 2

In Demonstration 1, the subclasses of the Luxury class (Gym and SwimmingPool) are very similar. In fact, those were stateless decorators that I used to represent fixed features. However, this need not be the case. In other words, you can use stateful decorators to represent customized features.

To illustrate, let us replace the SwimmingPool class with the following one:

```
using Ch01.Decorator.Home;
using static System.Console;

namespace Ch01.Decorator.Facilities
{
   public class SwimmingPoolParameterized (IHome home,PoolType poolType)
      : Luxury(home)
   {
      private readonly PoolType _poolType = poolType;
```

```
        public override void Create()
        {
            base.Create();
            PerformAdditionalCheck();
            WriteLine($"One {_poolType.ToString().ToLowerInvariant()} " +
              $"swimming pool is now made.");
        }

        private void PerformAdditionalCheck()
        {
            WriteLine("Checking whether a swimming pool can be added...");
        }
    }
}
```

Here, the PoolType is an enum that is defined as follows:

```
namespace Ch01.Decorator.Facilities
{
    public enum PoolType
    {
        Indoor,
        Rooftop
    }
}
```

POINT TO NOTE

I have used an enum type instead of strings such as "Indoor" or "Rooftop". To ensure type-safety, this is often considered a better practice. Why? If a developer accidentally passes "Indor" instead of "Indoor", there will be no compile-time error, and the mistake may remain unnoticed until runtime. It also makes refactoring easy, if you'd like to incorporate a small change; for example, "Rooftop" swimming pool to something else, such as "High-rise" swimming pool or "Elevated" swimming pool in the future. Finally, any powerful IDE can easily show the available options for you while coding.

```
using Ch01.Decorator.Facilities;
using Ch01.Decorator.Home;
using static System.Console;

namespace Ch01.Decorator.Demo2
{
    public class DecoratorDemo2
    {
        public static void Main()
        {
            IHome home = new BasicHome();
            home.Create();
            WriteLine("=========");

            // Adding a gym
            home = new Gym(home);
            home.Create();
            WriteLine("=========");

            // Adding indoor swimming pool
            home = new SwimmingPoolParameterized(home, PoolType.Indoor);
            home.Create();
            WriteLine("=========");

            // Adding rooftop swimming pool
            home = new SwimmingPoolParameterized(home, PoolType.Rooftop);
            home.Create();
        }
    }
}
```

Author's Note: Since all demonstrations in this chapter are organized inside the same project, you may need to change the startup object before running a particular demonstration. To do this, follow the path: **Right-click the Project ➤ Properties ➤ Application ➤ General**. Select the desired class from the **Startup object** dropdown as shown in Figure 1-8.

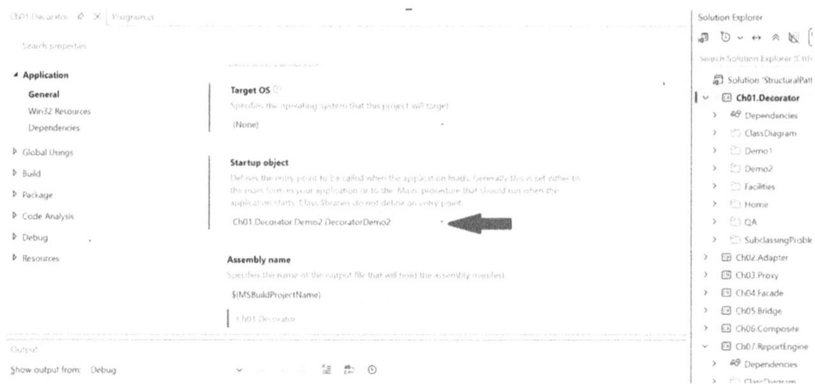

***Figure 1-8.** Preparing to run Demonstration 2 by selecting the startup object*

Output

Here is the new output:

```
A home with some basic facilities is made.
=========
A home with some basic facilities is made.
A gym is ready.
=========
A home with some basic facilities is made.
A gym is ready.
Checking whether a swimming pool can be added...
One indoor swimming pool is now made.
=========
A home with some basic facilities is made.
A gym is ready.
Checking whether a swimming pool can be added...
One indoor swimming pool is now made.
Checking whether a swimming pool can be added...
One rooftop swimming pool is now made.
```

Analysis

While forwarding a request to a component, a decorator can perform additional actions before or after forwarding. In this example, I performed the additional check **after** building the base home. If the check is a prerequisite, you can simply move the call **before** base.Create().

The addition of the PerformAdditionalCheck() method and the use of the PoolType enum (as explained in the Point to Note before) make our decorators both flexible and type-safe.

Finally, you can see that by passing the required parameters, I have avoided the use of multiple classes for swimming pools, such as IndoorSwimmingPool and RooftopSwimmingPool.

Q&A Session

Q1.1 You talked about the runtime composition of behavior in this design. You also claimed that it is better than inheritance in this example. Could you provide some further insight into this discussion?

When a derived class inherits from a base class, the structure of that inheritance hierarchy is fixed at compile time. Though runtime polymorphism is possible (using virtual methods), the combination of behaviors is determined by the class structure itself. So, this approach is relatively static compared to composition.

But by using composition, **you can combine behaviors at runtime by wrapping objects dynamically** (as in the previous example), which makes the design more flexible.

Notice that a decorator object is designed to have the same interface as the underlying object. It allows a client object to interact with the decorated object in the same way as it would with the underlying object. This is the reason: a decorator object contains a reference to the actual object. When a client sends a request, the decorated object forwards this request to the underlying object. But it can add functionality before or after forwarding the request to the actual object. This ensures that you add behavior at runtime without modifying the original object structure.

You must value this point. Why? While designing a parent class, you may not have enough visibility about what kind of additional responsibilities your clients may want in a later phase. Since the constraint is that you cannot modify the existing code, in this case, object composition not only outclasses inheritance but also ensures that you are not introducing bugs in the existing architecture.

Lastly, in this context, you may remember that one of the key design principles is *classes should be open for extension but closed for modification.*

KEY DISTINCTION

You can add, alter, or remove responsibilities by simply attaching or detaching decorators. But with simple inheritance techniques, you need to create new classes for new responsibilities. So, you may end up with a complex system. In this context, you can revisit the discussion of the subtopic- "Problem of Subclassing" under Implementation in this chapter.

Q1.2 What are the key advantages of using a decorator?

Here are some key advantages:

- Since you do not touch the existing structure, the possibility of introducing bugs in that part of the code is minimal.
- You can add a new functionality to an existing object easily. The same is true if you want to remove an unwanted functionality from the object as well.
- You can easily alter a behavior as per your needs.
- You do not need to predict/implement all the supported functionalities in the initial design phase. You can develop incrementally by adding decorators one by one. You must acknowledge that if you make a complex class first and then want to extend the functionalities, it will be a tedious process.

Q1.3 I notice that you have created the Gym class and the SwimmingPool classes with a single responsibility. Is this beneficial?

Yes. It makes the decorator pattern more efficient because you can simply add or remove a responsibility dynamically, one at a time.

Q1.4 What are the disadvantages associated with this pattern?

I believe that if you are careful, there are no significant disadvantages. But if you create too many decorators in the system, they can be hard to maintain and debug. This can create unnecessary complexity.

Q1.5 Is it mandatory to use decorators for dynamic behavior only?

No. You can use the concept for both static and dynamic binding. But dynamic binding is its strength, so I have concentrated on that here. The GoF definition also emphasized adding responsibilities dynamically.

Q1.6 I'd like to see an example: how can decorators promote static binding as well?

Let's make the following class:

Author's Note: You can find the following classes (AdvancedHome.cs and StaticDecoratorDemo.cs) in a separate namespace (Ch01.Decorator.QA):

```
using Ch01.Decorator.Facilities;
using Ch01.Decorator.Home;

namespace Ch01.Decorator.QA
{
  public class AdvancedHome(IHome home)
    : SwimmingPool(new Gym(home))
  {

  }
}
```

Now you can exercise the following code:

```
using Ch01.Decorator.Home;

namespace Ch01.Decorator.QA
{
  public class StaticDecoratorDemo
  {
    public static void Main()
    {
      IHome home = new AdvancedHome(new BasicHome());
      home.Create();
    }
  }
}
```

This time, you will see the following output:

```
A home with some basic facilities is made.
A gym is ready.
One swimming pool is made.
```

Author's Note: While analyzing the program, it is important to distinguish between the construction and execution of this program:

Note that in the construction phase, the "inner" object (**Gym**) is instantiated first because it is needed as an argument for the "outer" object (**SwimmingPool**).

However, in the execution phase, when home.Create() is called, the call starts from the outermost decorator (**SwimmingPool**), which then delegates the call to the wrapped object using base.Create(). As a result, the call travels down to the innermost core (**BasicHome**) before any messages are printed. This results in the "bottom-up" appearance of the output.

It is no surprise that you can reverse the order of gym and swimming pool creation by considering the following code (the old code is shown in a comment for your reference):

```
public class AdvancedHome(IHome home)
    //: SwimmingPool(new Gym(home))
    :Gym(new SwimmingPool(home))
{

}
```

However, in each case, this program statically incorporates the decorator composition into the type hierarchy.

Q1.7 I'd like to see an example: how can I remove a decorator dynamically at runtime?

Let's make some changes in Demonstration 1. First, I add a getter inside the Luxury class that you saw in Demonstration 1 as follows:

```
using Ch01.Decorator.Home;

namespace Ch01.Decorator.Facilities
{
```

```
    public abstract class Luxury(IHome home) : IHome
    {
        protected readonly IHome _home = home;

        public virtual void Create()
        {
            _home.Create();
        }

        /// <summary>
        /// Added for Q&A to show dynamic removal of decorators
        /// </summary>
        /// <returns></returns>
        public IHome GetInnerHome() => _home;

        //// Same as:
        //public IHome GetInnerHome()
        //{
        //    return _home;
        //}
    }
}
```

Now you can add a few lines of code (shown in bold) in DecoratorDemo1.cs to verify the effect of these changes. However, instead of making the changes directly in the same file, I created another file named DecoratorRemovalDemo.cs so that, if needed, you can easily run the program with these changes. Let's see the updated content now:

```
// DecoratorRemovalDemo.cs

using Ch01.Decorator.Home;
using Ch01.Decorator.Facilities;
using static System.Console;
```

```
namespace Ch01.Decorator.QA
{
    public class DecoratorRemovalDemo
    {
        public static void Main()
        {
            IHome home = new BasicHome();
            home.Create();
            WriteLine("=========");

            // Adding a gym
            home = new Gym(home);
            home.Create();
            WriteLine("=========");

            // Adding a swimming pool
            home = new SwimmingPool(home);
            home.Create();
            WriteLine("=========");

            #region Added for Q&A
            WriteLine("Removing the swimming pool from " +
                "the outer layer (if any) ...");
            if (home is SwimmingPool pool)
            {
                home = pool.GetInnerHome(); // Using pattern matching
            }
            home.Create();

            WriteLine("=========");


            #endregion
        }
    }
}
```

ALTERNATIVE CODE

In the previous code segment, by following Visual Studio's suggestion, I used pattern matching to remove a swimming pool from a home. Here is an alternative code to do the same:

```
#region Alternative code to remove the swimming pool from the outer layer
if (home is SwimmingPool)
{
  // Unwrap to get the inner home
  home = ((SwimmingPool)home).GetInnerHome();
}
home.Create();
#endregion
```

Upon executing the program, you will see the following output:

```
A home with some basic facilities is made.
=========
A home with some basic facilities is made.
A gym is ready.
=========
A home with some basic facilities is made.
A gym is ready.
One swimming pool is made.
=========
Removing the swimming pool from the outer layer (if any) ...
A home with some basic facilities is made.
A gym is ready.
=========
```

You can see that the swimming pool is removed from the home at runtime at the end of the output.

Q1.8 It would be helpful if you could explain how BufferedStream acts as a decorator in C#.

Consider the following code segment, which you may have already seen quite often:

```
namespace Ch01.Decorator.QA
{
  class BuiltInDecoratorDemo
  {
    public static void Main()
    {
      Stream stream = new FileStream("somefile.txt", FileMode.Create);
      stream = new BufferedStream(stream);
      // Some other code
    }
  }
}
```

Author's Note: In modern **.NET** projects (particularly, .NET 6 and later), namespaces such as **System.IO** are often imported automatically through implicit global using directives. Because of this, you do not see me showing using System.IO namespace to access classes like **Stream**, **FileStream**, or **BufferedStream** at the beginning of the file. However, in older projects or when implicit usings are disabled, you may need to add this directive manually.

You may note that the FileStream class inherits from the Stream class. Here is a sample code segment for your immediate reference:

```
namespace System.IO
{
  public class FileStream : Stream
  {
   // The remaining code is not shown here.
  }
}
```

Now focus on the BufferedStream class. Upon investigating, you'll see the following:

```
namespace System.IO
{
  // The intermediate documentation comments are skipped here
  public sealed class BufferedStream : Stream
    {
      private Stream? _stream;  // Underlying stream.  Close sets _stream to null.
      // Some code are skipped here
      public BufferedStream(Stream stream)
         : this(stream, DefaultBufferSize)
      {
      }
     public BufferedStream(Stream stream, int bufferSize)
     {
         // The remaining code is skipped here.
```

Now you can see that the BufferedStream class inherits from the Stream class, contains a field of type **Stream** (_stream), and has a constructor to accept a Stream object to store the object internally.

This BufferedStream object can now forward read and write operations to the underlying stream while adding buffering functionality.

For example, you can see the following:

```
public override void Write(byte[] buffer, int offset, int count)
{
  // The intermediate code is skipped here

  // Write out user data.
  _stream.Write(buffer, offset, count);
}
```

Now, if you compare our demonstration with this built-in example, you will find the following mapping:

- The IHome interface plays the role of the Stream.
- The BasicHome plays the role of FileStream (the concrete class that inherits from an abstract class).
- The Gym and SwimmingPool classes play the role of BufferedStream (a concrete decorator).

Though .NET does not use a separate abstract decorator layer similar to Luxury in our example, the concept of the Decorator pattern is still applied.

Summary

The Decorator pattern offers a flexible and extensible alternative to subclassing through object composition. It allows responsibilities to be added or removed dynamically, without requiring modifications to existing code. This makes the pattern especially useful when enhancing legacy systems, supporting varying client requirements, or adhering to the Open–Closed Principle. However, excessive use of decorators can make a system harder to understand because behavior becomes distributed across multiple small classes.

CHAPTER 2

Adapter Pattern

In real-world systems, you often encounter classes whose interfaces do not match what the clients expect. The Adapter pattern helps you bridge the gap and enables incompatible classes to work together.

Concept

The Gang of Four (GoF) defined the intent of the Adapter pattern as follows:

> *Convert the interface of a class into another interface clients expect. Adapter lets classes work together that couldn't otherwise because of incompatible interfaces.*

POINT TO NOTE

Interestingly, the Adapter pattern also uses wrapping, though its intent is interface adaptation rather than behavior extension (as in the Decorator pattern)

In a domain-specific system, the clients know how to invoke methods in the software. Those methods typically follow a specific interface or inheritance hierarchy. Now, assume the existing system needs to evolve and you need to integrate a third-party library. However, this library exposes a slightly different interface that you can use but cannot modify.

In this case, you do not want to force your clients to learn a new way to access the software. So, what can you do? The solution is simple: you can write an adapter that accepts client requests and translates these requests into a form that the third-party classes can understand. As a result, clients can enjoy the updated software without any hassle.

V. Sarcar, *The Structural Design Toolkit for C#*, https://doi.org/10.1007/979-8-8688-3029-7_2

In essence, the Adapter pattern enables two incompatible interfaces to collaborate by introducing an intermediary adapter.

POINT TO NOTE

There are two types of adapters: **object adapters (based primarily on composition)** and **class adapters (based primarily on inheritance)**. Both are covered in this chapter.

Real-Life Example

A common use of this pattern is when you use an electrical outlet adapter/AC power adapter during international travel. These adapters can act as middlemen so that an electronic device, say a laptop that is designed for a US power outlet, can be plugged into a European power outlet.

Even a translator who is converting one language to another can be considered an example of this pattern in real life.

Computer World Example

Suppose you have an application that can be broadly classified into two parts: the user interface (UI, the front end) and the database (the back end). Through the user interface, clients can pass some specific type of data or objects. Your database is compatible with those objects and can store them smoothly. Over time, you may realize that you need to upgrade your software to keep your clients happy. Therefore, you may want to allow other types of objects to pass through the UI. But in this case, the first issue will come from your database, because it cannot store those new objects. In such a situation, you can use an adapter that will take care of converting these new objects into a form compatible with the existing database. (To illustrate, you may consider a typical scenario: the UI provides **JSON** data, but the legacy database accepts only **XML**. This immediately makes the need for translation clear to the developer.)

In the .NET world, a common example is the use of classes that adapt older APIs to newer ones. For instance, when working with streams, classes like StreamReader and StreamWriter adapt a byte stream (Stream) to a character-based interface, enabling clients to work with text data more conveniently. These can be viewed as examples of object adapters. You will learn about class adapters and object adapters shortly.

Author's Note: Modern C# also provides lightweight, adapter-like behavior through extension methods in LINQ. For example, AsEnumerable() allows an array to be treated as an IEnumerable<T> without copying data. However, unlike StreamReader or StreamWriter, this is not a full-fledged object adapter; rather, it represents a minimal interface adaptation with little or no additional behavior.

POINT TO NOTE

In the previous chapter (see Q1.8), while both BufferedStream and StreamReader wrap an underlying Stream, their intents differ. BufferedStream enhances the existing interface by adding buffering (Decorator), whereas StreamReader converts a byte-based stream into a character-based interface (Adapter).

Implementation

The Adapter pattern can serve our needs with minor adjustments. To illustrate, let's begin with the following inheritance hierarchy, which includes four participants: IPersonInfo, Person, Student, and Teacher. In this hierarchy:

- Person implements IPersonInfo.
- Student and Teacher inherit from Person.
- As a result, all concrete classes are of type IPersonInfo.

Let's look into them sequentially:

POINT TO NOTE

This hierarchy reflects a typical educational organization consisting of students and teachers. For simplicity, let's assume that each person (i.e., a student or a teacher) has a name, age, and an identification number (ID).

You may also note that the same hierarchy will be used in both demonstrations in this chapter. Therefore, it is placed in Ch02.Adapter.Common namespace.

IPersonInfo is an interface that sits at the top of this hierarchy. It is defined as follows:

```
namespace Ch02.Adapter.Common
{
  // This is the target interface
  public interface IPersonInfo
  {
    string GetPersonDetails();
  }
}
```

Person is an abstract class that implements IPersonInfo. This class is basically used to contain the common code that its subclasses can use. Here is the Person class:

```
namespace Ch02.Adapter.Common
{
  public abstract class Person(string name, int age, string id) : IPersonInfo
  {
    protected string _name = name;
    protected int _age = age;
    protected string _id = id;

    public string GetPersonDetails()
    {
      return "Name: " + _name +
             ", Age: " + _age +
             ", ID: " + _id;
    }

    // The following properties will be used in
    //  the class adapter (Demo2)
    public string Name => _name;
    public int Age => _age;
    public string IdentificationNumber => _id;
  }
}
```

Author's Note: To avoid direct instantiation of the Person class, it is marked abstract. In addition, GetPersonDetails() is intentionally kept non-virtual because all subclasses share the same formatting logic in this demonstration.

The Student class inherits from the Person class and is defined as follows:

POINT TO NOTE

Student IDs are generated by prefixing a randomly generated number with "S_". For teachers, the prefix "T_" is used instead. This ID-generation logic is intentionally simplified and is not central to the discussion of the Adapter pattern in this chapter.

```
// Student.cs
namespace Ch02.Adapter.Common
{
  public class Student(string name, int age) : Person(name, age, GenerateId())
  {
    private static readonly Random random = new();
    private static string GenerateId()
    {
      int number = random.Next(1, 1000);
      return "S_" + number;
    }
  }
}
```

The Teacher class is similar to the Student class, differing only in ID generation. It is defined as follows:

```
namespace Ch02.Adapter.Common
{
  public class Teacher(string name, int age) : Person(name, age, GenerateId())
  {
    private static readonly Random random = new();
    private static string GenerateId()
```

```
        {
            int number = random.Next(1, 100);
            return "T_" + number;
        }
    }
}
```

The following client code demonstrates that all participants can be treated uniformly as IPersonInfo objects (I've simplified the collection initialization here; the alternative code is shown in comments):

Author's Note: The [] syntax used here is called a **collection expression,**[1] introduced in C# 12.[2] It is equivalent to creating a collection using new List<T>() and then adding elements manually. This syntax improves readability and reduces boilerplate code.

// Adapter.Demo1.cs

```
using Ch02.Adapter.Common;
using Ch02.Adapter.External;
// The following namespace is available by default, but shown here for clarity
using System.Collections.Generic;
using static System.Console;

namespace Ch02.Adapter.Demo1
{
    public class AdapterDemo1
    {
        public static void Main()
        {
            //WriteLine("Exercising an object adapter.");
            // Simplified collection initialization
            List<IPersonInfo> people =
            [   new Student("Sam", 25)
              , new Student("Bob", 21)
```

[1] https://learn.microsoft.com/en-us/dotnet/csharp/language-reference/operators/collection-expressions

[2] https://learn.microsoft.com/en-us/dotnet/csharp/whats-new/csharp-12

```
            , new Teacher("Jack", 45)
            ];

           #region Alternative code
           //List<IPersonInfo> people = new();
           //people.Add(new Student("Sam", 25));
           //people.Add(new Student("Bob", 21));
           //people.Add(new Teacher("Jack", 45));
           #endregion

           // Getting the details
           foreach (IPersonInfo person in people)
           {
              WriteLine(person.GetPersonDetails());
           }
        }
    }
}
```

This program can successfully execute and print the details. Here is a sample:

```
Name: Sam, Age: 25, ID: S_849
Name: Bob, Age: 21, ID: S_907
Name: Jack, Age: 45, ID: T_20
```

Note You may see a slightly different output on your computer because the IDs are generated at random.

So far, our application operates entirely within the IPersonInfo hierarchy.

Third-Party Code

Now, assume that we want to integrate a third-party system that represents people differently.

To illustrate, let's assume that someone has also developed a system that can print the details of a person who belongs to different professions. The Profession interface sits at the top of this hierarchy as follows:

// Profession.cs

```
namespace Ch02.Adapter.External
{
  public interface IProfession
  {
    string Name { get; }
    int Age { get; }
    string GetProfessionDetails();
  }
}
```

POINT TO NOTE

Notice that GetProfessionDetails() is a method, but not a property. Why this design choice? I'll use it to format and return derived information rather than exposing a simple value. In simple words, it represents behavior rather than simple data.

For simplicity, let us consider only musicians now. Here, the Musician class implements the IProfession interface as follows:

// Musician.cs

```
namespace Ch02.Adapter.External
{
  public class Musician(string name, int age) : IProfession
  {
    private readonly string _name = name;
    private readonly int _age = age;
    private readonly string _occupation = "Musician";

    public string Name => _name;
    public int Age => _age;
```

```
        public string GetProfessionDetails()
        {
            return $"Name: {_name}, Age: {_age}, Occupation: {_occupation}";
        }
    }
}
```

Understanding the Need

After reviewing the third-party code, you realize you could reuse it to print a musician's details as well. However, there is a constraint: although you can use the third-party code, you cannot introduce changes to that code. In such situations, you can use an adapter.

Author's Note: In discussions of the Adapter pattern, the incompatible interfaces are often referred to as the **target** and **adaptee** interfaces. In our example, since the client wants to print the details of the musician now, along with the existing teachers and students, IPersonInfo is the **target interface**, and IProfession is the **adaptee interface**.

The GoF described two types of adapters: class adapters and object adapters. In Demonstration 1, you'll see an object adapter. Demonstration 2 will cover the other one.

Table 2-1 can help you visualize the big picture before you focus on individual players.

Table 2-1. *Key Participants in the Adapter Pattern Demonstrations*

Role	Component	Purpose
Target Interface	IPersonInfo	The interface that the client already knows and uses.
Adaptee Interface	IProfession	The external or third-party code that has the data we need, but can have a different method name.

(continued)

Table 2-1. (*continued*)

Role	Component	Purpose
Adapter	ProfessionObjectAdapter (will be used in Demonstration 1) and ProfessionClassAdapter (will be used in Demonstration 2)	The "middleman" that connects the incompatible interfaces—IPersonInfo and IProfession.
Client	AdapterDemo1 (will be used in Demonstration 1) and AdapterDemo2 (will be used in Demonstration 2)	The class that needs to process objects.

Object Adapter

Object adapters adapt interfaces through object composition. You'll typically notice the following code structure in an object adapter:

- It **implements** the target interface IPersonInfo.
- It **holds** the adaptee instance (IProfession).
- It **accepts** the adaptee as a constructor argument to make use of composition.

Here is a sample implementation for you:

```
// ProfessionObjectAdapter.cs

using Ch02.Adapter.Common;
using Ch02.Adapter.External;

namespace Ch02.Adapter.Demo1
{
   public class ProfessionObjectAdapter(IProfession profession) : IPersonInfo
   {
      private readonly IProfession _profession = profession;

      public string GetPersonDetails()
```

```
        {
            return _profession.GetProfessionDetails();
        }
    }
}
```

Notice the beauty of using the adapter: you do not need to modify the third-party code. When the client calls the GetPersonDetails() method at a high level, that call internally delegates to GetProfessionDetails() of the wrapped IProfession object.

Class Diagram

Before you see the updated client code (**AdapterDemo1.cs**), let me show you the class diagram in Figure 2-1.

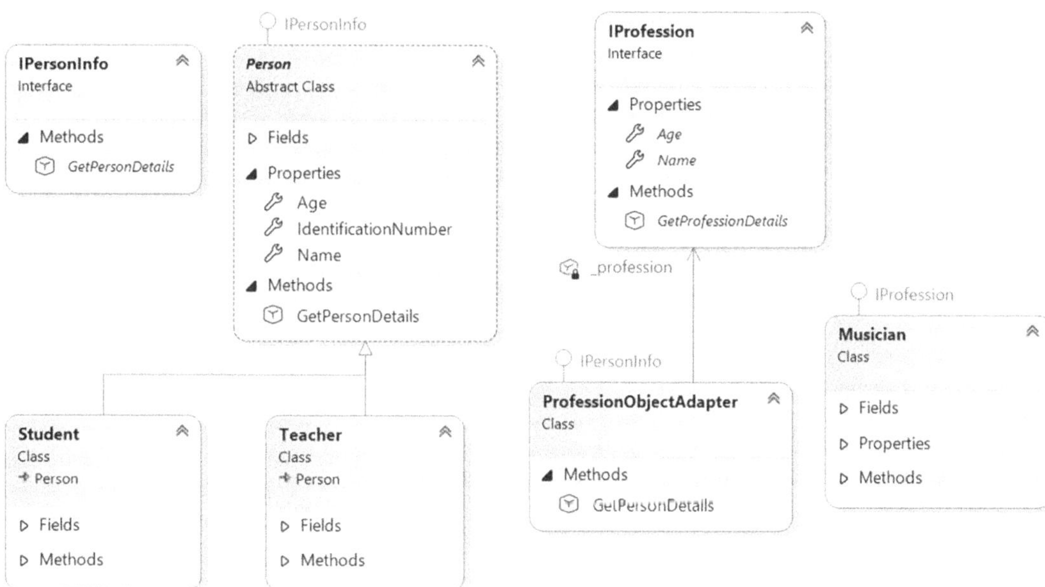

***Figure 2-1.** The object adapter used in Demonstration 1*

Author's Note: To keep the diagram short and simple, I have shown only the key properties and methods, along with their relationships.

Demonstration 1

The following is an updated version of the same client that uses the adapter now. Notice the key changes in bold. (I have also kept the alternative code for your immediate reference in the comment):

// AdapterDemo1.cs (Updated)

```
using Ch02.Adapter.Common;
using Ch02.Adapter.External;
// The following namespace is available by default, but shown here for clarity
using System.Collections.Generic;
using static System.Console;

namespace Ch02.Adapter.Demo1
{
    public class AdapterDemo1
    {
        public static void Main()
        {
            // Simplified collection initialization
            List<IPersonInfo> people =
            [  new Student("Sam", 25)
             , new Student("Bob", 21)
             , new Teacher("Jack", 45)
             // Using adapter now
             , new ProfessionObjectAdapter(new Musician("Kate", 30))
            ];

            #region Alternative code
            //List<IPersonInfo> people = new();
            //people.Add(new Student("Sam", 25));
            //people.Add(new Student("Bob", 21));
            //people.Add(new Teacher("Jack", 45));
            // Using adapter now
            //people.Add(new ProfessionObjectAdapter(new Musician
            ("Kate", 30)));
            #endregion
```

```
            // Getting the details
            foreach (IPersonInfo person in people)
            {
                WriteLine(person.GetPersonDetails());
            }
        }
    }
}
```

Output

Here is a sample output:

```
Name: Sam, Age: 25, ID: S_520
Name: Bob, Age: 21, ID: S_749
Name: Jack, Age: 45, ID: T_33
Name: Kate, Age: 30, Occupation: Musician
```

Class Adapter

Class adapters adapt through subclassing. They rely on multiple inheritance; however, since C# does not support multiple inheritance of classes, this effect is achieved by extending a concrete class and implementing one or more interfaces.

To illustrate, I'll now present an alternative implementation using a class adapter. It is as follows:

// ProfessionClassAdapter.cs

```
using Ch02.Adapter.Common;
using Ch02.Adapter.External;
namespace Ch02.Adapter.Demo2
{
    public class ProfessionClassAdapter(string name, int age)
        : Musician(name, age), IPersonInfo
    {
        public string GetPersonDetails()
        {
```

```
            return GetProfessionDetails();
        }
    }
}
```

Author's Note: The previous implementation uses a primary constructor. You have not yet seen me use a primary constructor in this type of multiple-inheritance-like implementation. So, let me show you the alternative version of it that does not use the primary constructor:

```
// The using statements and namespace details are
// not shown to avoid repetition

public class ProfessionClassAdapter : Musician, IPersonInfo
{
    public ProfessionClassAdapter(string name, int age) : base(name, age)
    {
    }
   public string GetPersonDetails()
   {
      return GetProfessionDetails();
   }
}
```

Class Diagram

Before you see the client code (**AdapterDemo2.cs**), let me show you the class diagram in Figure 2-2.

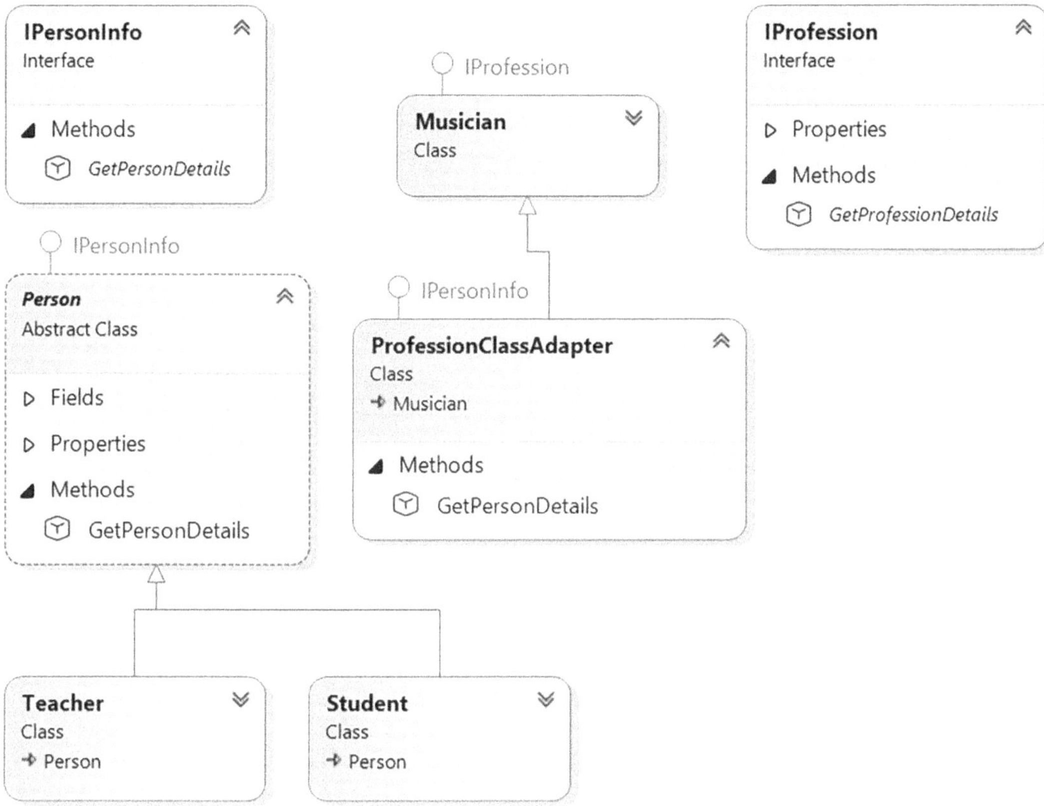

***Figure 2-2.** The class adapter used in Demonstration 2*

REMINDER

Figure 2-2 focuses on the key methods involved in adapting IProfession to IPersonInfo. Other details are not expanded for clarity.

Demonstration 2

Let's examine a sample client that can use this class adapter:

// AdapterDemo2.cs

```
using Ch02.Adapter.Common;
using Ch02.Adapter.External;
```

```
// The following namespace is available by default, but shown here for clarity
using System.Collections.Generic;
using static System.Console;

namespace Ch02.Adapter.Demo2
{
  public class AdapterDemo2
  {
    public static void Main()
    {
      WriteLine("Exercising a class adapter.");
      // Simplified collection initialization
      List<IPersonInfo> people =
        [ new Student("Sam", 25)
        , new Student("Bob", 21)
        , new Teacher("Jack", 45)
        ];
      Musician musician = new ("Kate", 30);

      // Using adapter now
      ProfessionClassAdapter adapter = new(musician.Name, musician.Age);
      people.Add(adapter);

      // Getting the details
      foreach (IPersonInfo person in people)
      {
        WriteLine(person.GetPersonDetails());
      }
    }
  }
}
```

Author's Note: In this demonstration, I created a Musician object explicitly to illustrate how information originating from a third-party type can be represented through a class adapter.

Output

Here is a sample output:

```
Exercising a class adapter.
Name: Sam, Age: 25, ID: S_642
Name: Bob, Age: 21, ID: S_43
Name: Jack, Age: 45, ID: T_95
Name: Kate, Age: 30, Occupation: Musician
```

Analysis

Notice that this output is similar to the output of Demonstration 1. The only difference is that this time, the demonstration uses a class adapter. As usual, the IDs are different because those were generated at random.

Interestingly, a class adapter can act as a two-way adapter. To illustrate, let's replace the previous code (**AdapterDemo2.cs**) with the following one. Here, I added a few lines of code to the previous code that are shown in bold:

Note I have kept this updated program in **AdapterDemo2Modified.cs** that can also be downloaded from the Apress website.

```
using Ch02.Adapter.Common;
using Ch02.Adapter.External;
// The following namespace is available by default, but shown here for clarity
using System.Collections.Generic;
using static System.Console;

namespace Ch02.Adapter.Demo2
{
    public class AdapterDemo2Modified
    {
        public static void Main()
        {
            WriteLine("Exercising a class adapter.");
            // Simplified collection initialization
```

```
        List<IPersonInfo> people =
          [ new Student("Sam", 25)
          , new Student("Bob", 21)
          , new Teacher("Jack", 45)
          ];
        Musician musician = new("Kate", 30);
        // Using adapter now
        ProfessionClassAdapter adapter = new(musician.Name, musician.Age);
        people.Add(adapter);

        // Getting the details
        foreach (IPersonInfo person in people)
        {
          WriteLine(person.GetPersonDetails());
        }
        #region added to show the two-way adapter
        WriteLine("\nAnalyzing the two-way adapter now.");
        UseTargetInterface(adapter);
        UseAdapteeInterface(adapter);
        #endregion
      }
      private static void UseTargetInterface(IPersonInfo personInfo)
      {
        WriteLine(personInfo.GetPersonDetails());
      }
      private static void UseAdapteeInterface(IProfession profession)
      {
        WriteLine(profession.GetProfessionDetails());
      }
    }
}
```

Upon executing this code, you will now see the following output (the changes are shown in bold):

```
Exercising a class adapter.
Name: Sam, Age: 25, ID: S_134
Name: Bob, Age: 21, ID: S_575
Name: Jack, Age: 45, ID: T_18
Name: Kate, Age: 30, Occupation: Musician

Analyzing the two-way adapter now.
Name: Kate, Age: 30, Occupation: Musician
Name: Kate, Age: 30, Occupation: Musician
```

This demonstrates that an instance of a class adapter can be used in two different scenarios. Here, you passed the adapter instance to the

- The UseTargetInterface(IPersonInfo personInfo) method that accepts an IPersonInfo instance (i.e., the target interface)
- The UseAdapteeInterface(IProfession profession) method that accepts an IProfession instance (i.e., the adaptee interface)

This "dual-role" capability is exactly what defines a two-way adapter. In this demonstration, the class adapter achieves this because it inherits from Musician (which implements IProfession) while simultaneously implementing the IPersonInfo interface.

However, this capability is limited to certain scenarios. For example, if the Musician class is sealed (i.e., it cannot be subclassed) or if IPersonInfo is a concrete class rather than an interface, this capability cannot be achieved.

Q&A Session

Q2.1 Which one do you prefer, class adapters or object adapters?

In most cases, I prefer object adapters because they are more flexible and rely on composition, rather than inheritance. Also, in many cases, it is challenging to implement a true class adapter when you need to adapt a specific method from the adaptee hierarchy, but there is no close match for it in the target interface.

We have also discussed the case when the adaptee class (e.g., Musician in our example) is concrete (or sealed) and the target is also a concrete class rather than an interface; you cannot inherit from it. In this case, the object adapter is the only viable solution.

Lastly, a class adapter can expose some unrelated methods (since it extends the adaptee and implements the target interface). These unrelated methods open up a possibility of misuse.

Q2.2 "...it is challenging to implement a true class adapter when you need to adapt a specific method from an adaptee hierarchy, but there is no close match for that in the target interface?" Can you please elaborate?

In my examples, the target interface methods and adaptee interface methods were similar. For example, in the IPersonInfo interface, I have the GetPersonDetails() method, and in the IProfession interface, I have the GetProfessionDetails() method. Why do they exist? They show the name and age of a person along with an ID (or profession). Right? Now, suppose there is a method called GetHobby() in IProfession, but there is no such method with similar functionality in IPersonInfo. In a case like this, if you need to adapt the GetHobby() method, you need to deeply analyze how to proceed. In real-world programming, a similar method can be much more complex and can have complex dependencies with other methods as well. So, if you do not have a corresponding target method, you may find challenges in adapting the method from an adaptee.

Q2.3 What happens if the target interface and the adaptee interface method signature differ?

It is not a big problem! If an adapter method has a few parameters, you can invoke the adaptee method with some additional dummy parameters (these can be derived, defaulted, or transformed parameters).

In the reverse scenario (if the adapter method has more parameters than the adaptee method), you can add some functionality using those additional parameters before transferring the call to the adaptee method.

In addition, if the method parameters are incompatible, you may need to use casting (if applicable and safe) as well.

POINT TO NOTE

Keep in mind that this pattern suits best when the objects involved are similar but not identical. In our demonstrations, the semantics of the discussed interfaces were close. For example, trying to adapt a circle into a rectangle would not make sense, as they represent unrelated abstractions.

Q2.4 It appears to me that you could instantiate the adaptee class directly inside the constructor of the object adapter class. Is this correct?

It can work, but it is not a preferred solution. In that case, your code will be tightly coupled. However, notice the object adapter that was used in Demonstration 1:

```
public class ProfessionObjectAdapter(IProfession profession) : IPersonInfo
{
   private readonly IProfession _profession = profession;

   // The remaining code is skipped
}
```

Using this construct, you can pass any implementation of IProfession to the adapter. This constructor injection promotes loose coupling, and you know that it is a better solution.

Q2.5 What are the drawbacks associated with this pattern?

The drawbacks are usually minor, though worth considering. First, you need to write and maintain additional adapter classes. Second, if an application requires numerous adapters to bridge multiple incompatible systems, the overall class count can grow, increasing the overall complexity of the system. Finally, an adapter introduces an additional level of indirection, which can sometimes make debugging slightly more involved as you step through the translation layer. Despite these minor concerns, the payoff is great—especially when integrating legacy or third-party systems that you cannot modify.

CODING TIPS

I suggest you make adapters as simple as possible. When you use class adapters, you may think that you can override the adaptee's behavior. But this practice is discouraged because, in that case, there is a behavior change between the adapter and the adaptee. This may create unnecessary challenges for anyone who needs to debug the code later.

Q2.6 Can you discuss a built-in C# example that demonstrates the Adapter pattern?

Consider the following program. Here, you see a class named Displayer. This class has a method called DisplayNames that accepts a List<string> instance, but the client has a string array of names. Can you invoke the method using this array of names? Yes, by using names.ToList() as an adapter, you can bridge this gap. Here is the complete program with the important line in bold:

// BuiltInAdapterDemo.cs

```
// The following using statements are shown for clarity.
// These were available by default in the project setup.

using System.Collections.Generic; // needed for List<string>
using System.Linq; // needed for ToList()
using static System.Console;

namespace Ch02.Adapter.QA
{
   class Displayer
   {
      public static void DisplayNames(List<string> names)
      {
         foreach (var name in names)
         {
            Write(name + "\t");
         }
      }
   }
   class BuiltInAdapterDemo
   {
      static void Main()
      {
         string[] names = { "Sam", "Jack", "Kate" };
         //Displayer.DisplayNames(names); //  Not allowed
```

```
            Displayer.DisplayNames(names.ToList()); // Adapter-like behavior
        }
    }
}
```

Now you understand that the String[] was the **incompatible type,** List<string> was the **client-expected type,** and names.ToList() provided **adapter-like behavior** by converting the array into the expected type.

Author's Note: I believe that AsEnumerable() is closer to a pure interface adaptation. However, ToList() provides a clearer demonstration of the concept of the Adapter pattern in C# because it introduces an explicit type mismatch that must be resolved.

Q2.7 Can you combine multiple patterns in an application?

Definitely. In fact, it is very common. In Demonstration 2 of Chapter 3, you'll see me combining decorator and proxy patterns to make an application. In **Part II** of this book, you'll see me combining all the patterns in this book to build a mini application as well.

Interestingly, you may also come across code similar to the following in C# applications:

```
// The OpenRead(..) method opens an existing file for reading
 Stream stream = File.OpenRead("Some_file.txt");
 BufferedStream bufferedStream = new(stream);
 StreamReader reader = new(bufferedStream);
```

Here, BufferedStream behaves like a decorator because it adds buffering behavior to an existing Stream, while StreamReader behaves like an adapter by converting a byte-based Stream into a character-based reader.

Although this is not a strict textbook combination of patterns, it demonstrates how multiple design patterns can collaborate in real-world frameworks.

Summary

The Adapter pattern can help you work with incompatible interfaces seamlessly. This chapter has covered this pattern with multiple demonstrations. Here, you learned about both object adapters and class adapters, along with their pros and cons. You have also seen how a class adapter can play the role of a two-way adapter.

CHAPTER 3

Proxy Pattern

There are situations where you want to restrict direct communication between an intended object and the outside world. There are various reasons for this. For example, you may need to enhance security, improve application response time, or address resource constraints. The Proxy pattern is used to handle those situations. This chapter discusses this pattern with sample implementations.

Concept

The Gang of Four (GoF) defined the intent of the Proxy pattern as follows:

> *Provide a surrogate or placeholder for another object to control access to it.*

Though proxies can be of different types, fundamentally, they are substitutes (or placeholders) for an original object. In practice, when a client interacts with a proxy object, it appears that it is directly talking to the actual object. So, using this pattern, you can create a class that acts as an interface-compatible layer for the original one.

POINTS TO REMEMBER

Proxies can be of different types. So, it is not surprising that, based on the demand, the implementations can be different. For example, **protection proxies** typically deal with access rights to control direct use of an object. On the contrary, **virtual proxies** are useful for constructing a complex or costly object on demand. For example, while running an application, you may not like to load a very large image unless it is truly required. This approach is also known as lazy initialization (or lazy loading). The **remote proxy** is another type of proxy, which is used to provide a local representation of a remote object.

V. Sarcar, *The Structural Design Toolkit for C#*, https://doi.org/10.1007/979-8-8688-3029-7_3

In this chapter, you will see a Proxy pattern implementation that will cover the ideas of a protection proxy and a virtual proxy. I assume that once you see these implementations, the idea of using a proxy will become clear. The discussion of other types of proxies is beyond the scope of this chapter.

Real-Life Example

Consider the case when a particular teacher in a school is absent due to some unavoidable circumstances. Then the school authority may send another teacher as a replacement to take the classes.

You can consider the example from a different domain, say ATMs. An ATM implementation can hold proxy objects for bank information that actually exists on a remote server.

Computer World Example

In the real programming world, creating multiple instances of a complex object can be costly. This is simply because you may need some resources that are not easily available (or allocatable). In such a situation, you can create multiple proxy objects that can reference the original object. This mechanism can help you save system memory and improve the performance of your application.

Another very common use of a proxy can be seen when a user does not want to disclose the true IP address of their machine and wants to browse anonymously.

Here are a few more examples:

- Earlier, .NET developers used to rely on Windows Communication Foundation (WCF) for service-oriented applications, which heavily utilized generated client proxies. In modern .NET, this has evolved: developers now use **gRPC client proxies** for high-performance, contract-first communication or implement the Proxy pattern manually using **typed HttpClient** instances for REST-based services.
- You can see this pattern in other domains too. For example, Java developers often use the java.rmi.* package through which an object on one Java virtual machine can invoke methods on an object that resides in a different Java virtual machine.

Implementation

It's time to see some implementations. Let's start.

Building a Proxy

Let's assume a typical corporate network that restricts access to certain websites. To implement this scenario, we can design a protection proxy. First, let's examine the current architecture.

It begins with the following interface:

```
namespace Ch03.Proxy.Common
{
    public interface IService
    {
        void Connect(string url);
    }
}
```

The NetworkService class implements this IService interface. To begin with, let's define a simple enumeration to represent different types of networks:

```
namespace Ch03.Proxy.Common
{
    public enum NetworkType
    {
        Corporate,
        Public
    }
}
```

Let me show you the NetworkService class now:

POINT TO NOTE

In this example, the NetworkService class is declared as internal to indicate that it is an implementation detail rather than part of the public API. This improves encapsulation by limiting its visibility and discouraging unintended direct usage. **Although it remains accessible within the same assembly, clients are expected to interact through the proxy so that additional behaviors—such as access control and lazy initialization—are applied consistently.** In real-world applications, this restriction can be enforced more strictly by separating components into different assemblies.

```
using Ch03.Proxy.Common;
using static System.Console;

namespace Ch03.Proxy.Common
{
  internal class NetworkService(NetworkType networkType) : IService
  {
    private readonly NetworkType _networkType = networkType;
    public void Connect(string url)
    {
      WriteLine($"A {_networkType.ToString().ToLowerInvariant()} user " +
          $"is trying to connect: " + url);
    }
  }
}
```

ServiceProxy is the proxy class in our example. Before you see this class, remember the following points:

- This class is declared public and placed in the Ch03.Proxy.Demo1 namespace (you may note that the NetworkService class was placed in the Ch03.Proxy.Common namespace).
- Though the NetworkService class is simple in our example, in a real-world scenario, instantiating such a class can involve complex operations. **So, I'd use the lazy initialization technique to create this object only when it is required.**

- In our implementation, the ServiceProxy class contains a method with the **same name**—Connect(string url)—and a client can use this method through a ServiceProxy instance. When a client calls this method on the proxy object, the call propagates to the Connect(string url) method of the NetworkService object. This gives clients a feeling that they have invoked the method on the actual object (an instance of NetworkService in our example) directly.

POINTS TO REMEMBER

In our example, the ServiceProxy class is used to restrict URLs to either "facebook.com" or "tiktok.com". **So, it acts as a protection proxy**. Since I use lazy initialization to instantiate NetworkService, **it also behaves as a virtual proxy**. This combined behavior is intentional and helps illustrate how a single proxy can serve multiple purposes in a real-world design.

Before I show you the proxy class, let me introduce an optional custom exception—AccessDeniedException, which is defined as follows:

```
namespace Ch03.Proxy.Common
{
   public class AccessDeniedException(string message) : Exception(message)
   {
   }
}
```

You should not find any difficulty in understanding the following proxy class (**ServiceProxy.cs**) now. Still, I have kept some supporting comments to make things easier for you:

Note In the previous chapter, you learned about the collection expression that is equivalent to creating a collection using new List<T>() and then adding elements manually. I have used it in the following code to simplify collection initialization as well.

// ServiceProxy.cs

```
using Ch03.Proxy.Common;
using static System.Console;

namespace Ch03.Proxy.Demo1
{
    public class ServiceProxy : IService
    {
        private IService? _service;
        private readonly NetworkType _networkType;
        public ServiceProxy(NetworkType networkType)
        {
            _networkType = networkType;
            // We'll NOT create the actual network service unless it is required.
            // This is the lazy initialization part of the virtual proxy pattern.
        }

        private static readonly List<string> _restrictedUrls =
        [
            "facebook.com",
            "tiktok.com"
            // Add other URLs, if needed
        ];

        public void Connect(string url)
        {
            // The logic for the protection proxy
            if (_networkType == NetworkType.Corporate)
            {
                string urlLowerCase = url.ToLowerInvariant();
                foreach (string restricted in _restrictedUrls)
                {
```

```
                if (urlLowerCase.Contains(restricted))
                {
                    throw new AccessDeniedException($"You cannot connect" +
                        $" to {url} as per company policy.");
                }
            }
        }

        // Lazy initialization: the virtual proxy is in action
        if (_service == null)
        {
            WriteLine("Initializing the real service now... ");
            _service = new NetworkService(_networkType);
        }

        _service.Connect(url);
    }
  }
}
```

Author's Note: For simplicity, this example uses substring matching instead of precise domain validation.

Class Diagram

Before I show you the client code (**ProxyDemo1.cs**), let's see the class diagram (Figure 3-1) as well.

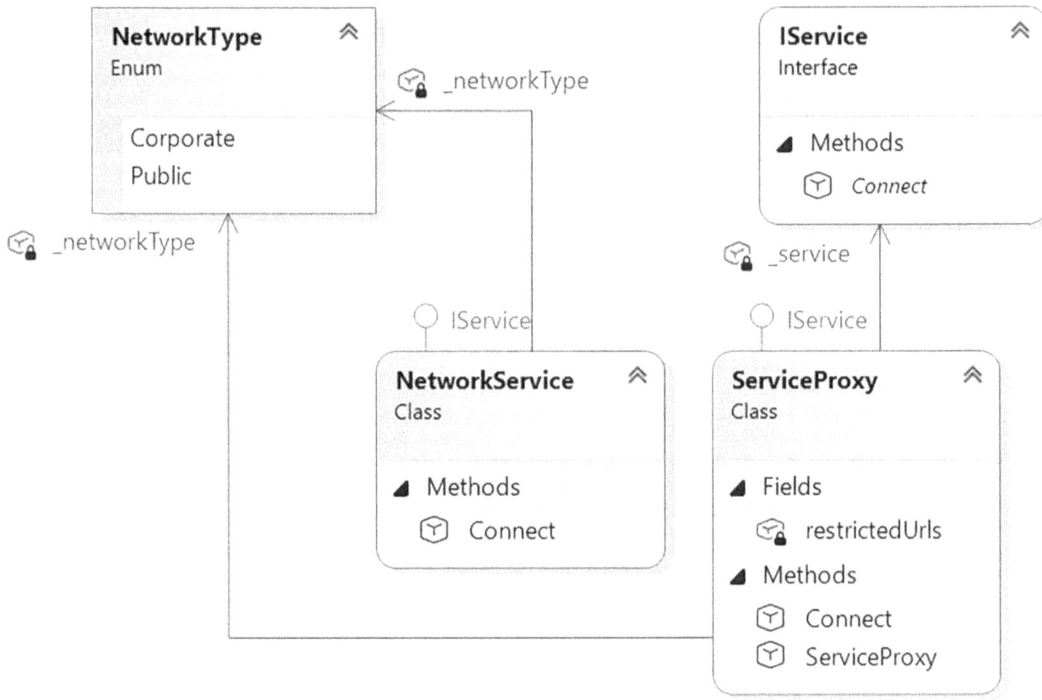

***Figure 3-1.** The key participants of Demonstration 1 are implementing the Proxy pattern*

Author's Note: For clarity, this class diagram focuses only on the key participants of the Proxy pattern. Remember that the NetworkType enumeration is a supporting configuration element rather than a structural participant. The client class (ProxyDemo1.cs) is not shown in this class diagram, as it only demonstrates usage and does not contribute to the core structure of the pattern.

Demonstration 1

Here is a sample client that uses our Proxy pattern implementation:

// ProxyDemo1.cs

```
using Ch03.Proxy.Common;
using static System.Console;
```

```
namespace Ch03.Proxy.Demo1
{
    class ProxyDemo1
    {
        public static void Main()
        {
            IService service = new ServiceProxy(NetworkType.Corporate);
            // This bypasses the proxy and should be avoided
            // IService service = new NetworkService(NetworkType.Corporate);
            try
            {
                // The following code should trigger the initialization
                service.Connect("https://google.com");
                // The following code should reuse the existing object
                service.Connect("https://yahoo.com");
                // The following code should block the connection
                service.Connect("https://www.facebook.com");
            }
            catch (AccessDeniedException e)
            {
                WriteLine(e.Message);
            }
        }
    }
}
```

Output

Here is a sample output:

```
Initializing the real service now...
A corporate user is trying to connect: https://google.com
A corporate user is trying to connect: https://yahoo.com
You cannot connect to https://www.facebook.com as per company policy.
```

Q&A Session

Q3.1 Using an unsynchronized lazy instantiation process in a multithreaded application can lead to race conditions and unnecessary object creation. Is this correct?

Correct. Do not forget that I used this simple illustration to convey the idea of the Proxy pattern. To handle this situation, you can synchronize the lazy initialization process as follows:

```
 #region To answer Q&A 3.1
 private readonly object _lock = new();
 public void Connect(string url)
 {
    lock (_lock)
    {
       // There is no change in the connection logic that you saw earlier
       // i.e., wrap the earlier connection logic inside this block
    }
}
#endregion
```

Author's Note: This implementation is intentionally simple and locks the entire method for clarity. In production code, developers often synchronize only the critical sections that require thread safety.

However, I want you to be aware of a potential drawback: a locking mechanism adds overhead and can impact performance. For a small application, the performance penalty can be negligible, but in high-concurrency systems, developers may look for alternative solutions.

In modern .NET, there are several improvements in handling concurrency and asynchronous programming, including the Task Parallel Library (TPL) and async/await constructs. For example, in high-concurrency scenarios, developers may consider applying double-checked locking or using thread-safe lazy initialization constructs (e.g., Lazy<T> in .NET).

Author's Note: While discussing the Singleton pattern in my other books, such as *Creational Design Patterns in C#* (Apress, 2025)[1] or *Design Patterns in C#* (2nd Edition, Apress, 2020),[2] I discussed various implementation techniques for the Singleton pattern.

Q3.2 Can you give an example of a remote proxy?

Suppose you need to invoke a method on an object that resides on a different computer. How can you achieve this? With the help of remote proxies, you can call the method on the proxy object, which in turn will forward the call to the actual object that is running on the remote machine (you can relate this to Demonstration 1 if the actual service resides on a different computer and is accessed via a proxy over a network). This type of communication can be implemented using modern technologies and frameworks such as ASP.NET Core and gRPC, as well as older technologies like CORBA, COM/DCOM, and Java RMI.

Let's look at Figure 3-2 that shows a simple remote proxy structure.

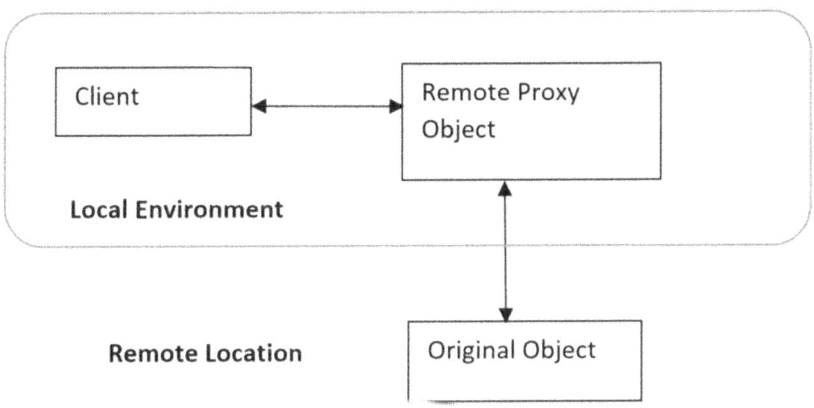

Figure 3-2. *A simple remote proxy diagram*

Q3.3 When can you use a virtual proxy?

They can be used to defer the creation of expensive objects. If the actual object creation is an expensive operation, you can use a lightweight placeholder for the intended object and supply it to the user. The expensive object will be created only when it is truly needed. You can use the concept to avoid unnecessarily loading an extremely large image to improve application performance.

[1] https://link.springer.com/book/10.1007/979-8-8688-1567-6

[2] https://link.springer.com/book/10.1007/978-1-4842-6062-3

Q3.4 It appears to me that proxy implementations are similar to decorators. Is this correct?

It is true that both the Proxy and Decorator patterns can compose an object and provide an identical interface to clients, but their intents are different. You need to focus on the purposes, not on any specific implementation.

Remember that decorators are used to add one or more responsibilities (most often dynamically), whereas proxies are primarily focused on controlling access to an intended object. Typically, you can think of a **proxy as a gatekeeper**, whereas you can consider a **decorator as an enhancer**. The following discussion will make things easier for you, as I add functionality to an existing proxy.

Adding a Decorator to a Proxy

In the previous demonstration, you saw how a proxy can control access to an object and delay its creation by acting as both a protection proxy and a virtual proxy. Let's enhance this proxy-based solution one step further by **combining it with the Decorator pattern**. While the proxy continues to manage access and object creation, a decorator is layered on top of the proxy to **add additional behavior without modifying the proxy.**

Demonstration 2

The following decorator is added to log some simple details before and after connecting to a URL:

```
// LoggingDecorator.cs

using static System.Console;

namespace Ch03.Proxy.Common
{
   public class LoggingDecorator(IService service) : IService
   {
      private readonly IService _service = service;

      public void Connect(string url)
      {
         WriteLine("[LOG] Attempting to access: " + url);
         _service.Connect(url);
         WriteLine("[LOG] Completed request for: " + url);
```

```
        }
    }
}
```

Here is a sample client:

```
// ProxyDemo2.cs

using Ch03.Proxy.Common;
using Ch03.Proxy.Demo1;
using static System.Console;

namespace Ch03.Proxy.Demo2
{
    public class ProxyDemo2
    {
        public static void Main()
        {
            // Trying to create a proxy
            IService service = new ServiceProxy(NetworkType.Corporate);
            // Decorating the proxy
            IService decoratedProxy = new LoggingDecorator(service);
            try
            {
                // The following code should trigger the initialization
                decoratedProxy.Connect("https://google.com");
                // The following code should reuse the existing object
                decoratedProxy.Connect("https://yahoo.com");
                // The following code should block the connection
                decoratedProxy.Connect("https://www.facebook.com");
            }
            catch (AccessDeniedException e)
            {
                WriteLine(e.Message);
            }
        }
    }
}
```

Output

Here is a sample output:

```
[LOG] Attempting to access: https://google.com
Initializing the real service now...
A corporate user is trying to connect: https://google.com
[LOG] Completed request for: https://google.com
[LOG] Attempting to access: https://yahoo.com
A corporate user is trying to connect: https://yahoo.com
[LOG] Completed request for: https://yahoo.com
[LOG] Attempting to access: https://www.facebook.com
You cannot connect to https://www.facebook.com as per company policy.
```

Q&A Session

Q3.5 When should I think of designing a proxy?

Here are some typical use cases where proxies can help you:

- You need to write test cases for a scenario that is still in the development phase or very hard to reproduce. To illustrate, let's assume you'd like to evaluate a particular behavior in an application that can only be observed in a customer environment. You also know that the probability of observing that behavior is very low. In such a case, you can mimic the customer environment behavior using a proxy object and execute your test cases to evaluate the correctness of that behavior.
- You want to hide the complexity and enhance the security of the system.

Author's Note: In modern testing terminology, developers often use terms such as mock, stub, fake, or test double to describe objects that simulate or control behavior during testing. Depending on the context, a proxy object can sometimes play a similar role.

Q3.6 What are the cons associated with proxies?

Here are some factors that you should keep in mind while using this pattern:

- The overall response time can be an issue because you are not directly talking to the actual object.
- You need to maintain an additional layer of proxies.
- Lastly, a proxy can hide the actual responses from objects. For example, if a proxy method modifies the original exception thrown by a method, debugging and fixing such a case is not always straightforward.

Q3.7 I have seen that you have discussed dynamic proxies in your other book *The Structural Design Toolkit for Java*.[3] Why is this absent here?

In Java, dynamic proxies can be created at runtime using the InvocationHandler interface. In .NET, similar behavior can be achieved using advanced techniques such as DispatchProxy or third-party libraries. However, these approaches are more complex and are typically used in frameworks rather than in everyday application code. To focus purely on the intent of the Proxy pattern, these details are avoided here.

Q3.8 Is a dynamic proxy a different type of proxy compared to a virtual or protection proxy?

No. Virtual and protection proxies describe why a proxy is used, whereas a dynamic proxy describes how a proxy is implemented. A dynamic proxy can be used to implement virtual, protection, or other proxies at runtime.

Summary

The Proxy pattern introduces a substitute object that controls, delays, or redirects access to a real object while keeping the client unchanged. This chapter showed two demonstrations to illustrate this pattern. The first one illustrated the idea of a protection proxy and a virtual proxy. The next demonstration showed how the Proxy pattern can be combined with the Decorator pattern to add additional behavior without altering the existing proxy.

[3] https://www.amazon.com/dp/B0GMKZD9NY

CHAPTER 4

Facade Pattern

The Facade pattern encourages loose coupling. Using this pattern, you emphasize abstraction and hide complex details by exposing a simple interface. This chapter explains this pattern with simple examples.

Concept

The Gang of Four (GoF) defined the intent of the Facade pattern as follows:

> *Provide a unified interface to a set of interfaces in a subsystem. Facade defines a higher-level interface that makes the subsystem easier to use.*

Consider an application that consists of multiple classes, each containing multiple methods. Assume that a client can make a product using a combination of methods from these classes. However, the problem is that the client needs to remember which classes to use, which methods to invoke, and the calling sequence of these methods. This may be acceptable for a developer, but it can make a client's life difficult. It can also be challenging if there is a lot of variation among these products.

To overcome this, you can use the Facade pattern. This pattern provides the client with a user-friendly, simple interface, so that all the internal complexities (such as which methods to invoke and what the calling sequence or series of steps should be) are hidden from the client. As a result, a client can concentrate on the final product only.

In short, facades provide a simplified entry point to a subsystem and coordinate interactions among its underlying components. Now, consider the following possibilities:

- You design the system so that a client cannot access the individual methods directly. Instead, you force them to access those methods through the facade only. In this case, the facade is called an **opaque facade**.
- Otherwise, it is a **transparent** facade.

V. Sarcar, *The Structural Design Toolkit for C#*, https://doi.org/10.1007/979-8-8688-3029-7_4

Interestingly, depending on the programming language, you can also make a top-level static class to prevent its instantiation. For example, though C# allows this, Java does not.

NOTE FOR JAVA DEVELOPERS

Java Language Specification (Java SE 25) (see https://docs.oracle.com/javase/specs/jls/se25/html/jls-8.html#jls-8.1.1) states that *the modifier static pertains only to member classes and local classes.*

Even though C# allows you to write a top-level static class, there are certain restrictions to follow. For example, you can use static data and methods only within a static class. So, depending on the programming language, you can make a top-level static class with static methods to avoid direct instantiation of a facade class. And when you use a similar concept, we say that you are using a **static** facade.

Real-World Example

Suppose you are planning to host a birthday party with a large number of guests. Nowadays, you can hire a party organizer and provide key information, such as the party type, date and time, number of attendees, and so on. The organizer will do the rest for you. You do not need to worry about how the organizer(s) will decorate the party room, manage the buffet service, and so on.

Computer World Example

Think about a case where you use a method from a library (in the context of a programming language). You don't worry about how the method is implemented in the library. You just call the method for ease of use.

In C#, the System.IO.File class provides a good example of the Facade pattern. Other classes, such as HttpClient, also exhibit facade-like characteristics by simplifying access to complex subsystems, although they are richer in functionality.

For example, the File class exposes methods like ReadAllText(), while internally working with streams and readers. The HttpClient class also provides simple methods like GetStringAsync(), but internally, it coordinates multiple lower-level components responsible for handling HTTP requests and responses. In both cases, the user interacts with a simplified interface without worrying about the underlying complexity.

The upcoming demonstration will make the concept clearer to you.

Implementation

It's time to see some implementations. In this chapter, I'll discuss two cases. The first case is as follows.

Simplifying Internal Subsystems

Consider a case when a customer applies for a loan from a bank. The bank officials must do some background verification before granting the loan to the customer. This background verification is a complex process that consists of various subprocesses. If a customer satisfies all the criteria, the loan can be approved. However, the customer is unaware of the background verification process conducted by the bank. In the following example, we'll try to mimic the process.

For simplicity, let's make the following assumptions for approving a loan:

- The loan applicants must have some assets. If the asset value is less than the claimed loan amount, they cannot get the loan.
- If applicants have an existing loan, they cannot get any new loan.
- If the above conditions do not apply to customers, they can get a loan.

Our job is to make an application that is based on these assumptions. Here are some examples for better clarity:

Case-1:
Bob's current asset value is $5000.
He claims a loan amount of $20,000.
He has an existing loan.

Expected Outcome: The loan cannot be approved due to the following reasons:

- Bob's asset value is insufficient (i.e., less than the claimed amount).
- Bob has an existing loan that prevents him from getting a new loan.

Case-2:

Jack's current asset value is $70,000.
He claims a loan amount of $30,000.
He has no existing loan.

Expected Outcome: Jack can get the loan. It is because his asset value is more than the claim amount, and he does not have any existing loans.

Case-3:

Tony's current asset value is $125,000.
He claims a loan amount of $50,000.
He has an existing loan.

Expected Outcome: Tony cannot get the loan because he has an existing loan.

Let us build the application now.

As per the requirement, in the upcoming example, you will see four classes—Person, Asset, ExistingLoanChecker, and LoanApprover (serving as the facade). A Person object can apply for a loan. This class has a constructor that takes three parameters: name, assetValue, and hasExistingLoan. Here is the Person class:

// Person.cs

```
namespace Ch04.Facade.Demo1
{
    public class Person
    {
        public string Name { get; }
        public double AssetValue { get; }
        public bool HasExistingLoan { get; }
```

```
        public Person(string name, double assetValue, bool hasExistingLoan)
        {
            Name = name;
            AssetValue = assetValue;
            HasExistingLoan = hasExistingLoan;
        }
        public override string ToString()
        {
            return $"[Name: {Name}, " +
                   $"current asset: {AssetValue}, " +
                   $"existing loan? {HasExistingLoan}]";
        }
    }
}
```

Now see the Asset class. This class has a method HasSufficientAssetValue, to verify whether the current asset value is greater than or equal to the claim amount. Here is the Asset class:

```
// Asset.cs

using static System.Console;

namespace Ch04.Facade.Demo1
{
    public class Asset
    {
        public bool HasSufficientAssetValue(Person person, double claimAmount)
        {
            WriteLine($"Verifying {person.Name}'s asset value.");
            return person.AssetValue >= claimAmount;
        }
    }
}
```

POINT TO NOTE

Although Asset and ExistingLoanChecker (you'll see it shortly) classes are currently **stateless**, I have modeled them as **instance-based classes** and invoked their **instance methods**. I could have used static methods in one or both classes, but that would have been a design preference, not a requirement. I believe that using instance objects avoids confusion and matches real-world scenarios where these subsystems might later hold state.

Now see the ExistingLoanChecker class. This class has a method HasExistingLoan, to verify whether a person has an existing loan.

```
// ExistingLoanChecker.cs

using static System.Console;

namespace Ch04.Facade.Demo1
{
   public class ExistingLoanChecker
   {
      public bool HasExistingLoan(Person person)
      {
         WriteLine($"Verifying whether {person.Name} has an existing loan.");
         return person.HasExistingLoan;
      }
   }
}
```

Finally, here is the facade:

POINT TO NOTE

In the following class, you'll see me instantiating the Asset and ExistingLoanChecker classes inside the CheckLoanEligibility method for simplicity and clarity in this demonstration. In a real-world high-performance application, I would prefer to move these instantiations to the constructor and reuse the objects to save memory and CPU cycles. However, for this demonstration, creating them inside the method keeps the focus on how the Facade pattern can coordinate with the subsystems.

```
// LoanApprover.cs

using static System.Console;

namespace Ch04.Facade.Demo1
{
    public class LoanApprover
    {
        public string CheckLoanEligibility(Person person, double claimAmount)
        {
            string status = "Approved";
            string reason = "";
            WriteLine("\nChecking the loan approval status of a person...");
            WriteLine($"{person} claims: ${claimAmount}");

            Asset asset = new();
            ExistingLoanChecker existingLoanChecker = new();

            if (!asset.HasSufficientAssetValue(person, claimAmount))
            {
                status = "Not approved.";
                reason += "\n The current asset value is insufficient.";
            }

            if (existingLoanChecker.HasExistingLoan(person))
            {
                status = "Not approved.";
                reason += "\n An existing loan prevents approval.";
            }

            string result = status;
            if (status != "Approved")
            {
                // Collecting the remarks (if any).
                result = status + "\nReason(s): " + reason;
            }
            return result;
        }
    }
}
```

Class Diagram

Before you see the client code (**FacadeDemo1.cs**), let us see the class diagram in Figure 4-1 as well.

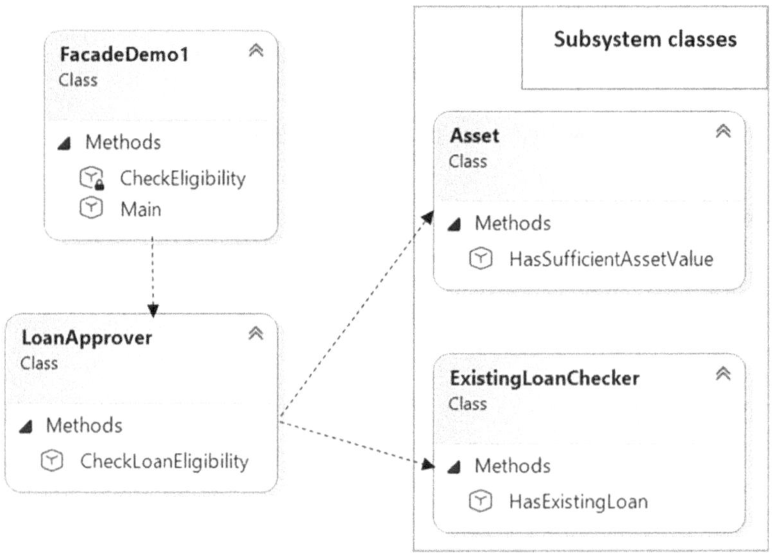

Figure 4-1. *Key participants in Demonstration 1*

Author's Note: I have omitted the domain object—Person from this diagram. It is because I want you to focus on the core intent of the Facade pattern rather than the complete object model.

Demonstration 1

Let's analyze three loan applicants—Bob, Jack, and Tony—with the following client code:

// FacadeDemo1.cs

```
using static System.Console;

namespace Ch04.Facade.Demo1
{
   public class FacadeDemo1
   {
      public static void Main()
      {
```

```
            WriteLine("***Simplifying the usage of a complex system using a facade.***");

            // Using a facade
            LoanApprover loanApprover = new ();

            // Person-1
            Person person = new ("Bob", 5000, true);
            CheckEligibility(person, 20000, loanApprover);
            WriteLine("--------");

            // Person-2
            person = new ("Jack", 70000, false);
            CheckEligibility(person, 30000, loanApprover);
            WriteLine("--------");

            // Person-3
            person = new ("Tony", 125000, true);
            CheckEligibility(person, 50000, loanApprover);
            WriteLine("--------");
        }
        private static void CheckEligibility(
            Person person,
            double claimAmount,
            LoanApprover approver)
        {
            string approvalStatus = approver.CheckLoanEligibility(person, claimAmount);
            WriteLine($"{person.Name}'s application status: {approvalStatus}");
        }
    }
}
```

Output

Here's the output:

```
***Simplifying the usage of a complex system using a facade.***
```

```
Checking the loan approval status of a person...
[Name: Bob, current asset: 5000, existing loan? True] claims: $20000
Verifying Bob's asset value.
Verifying whether Bob has an existing loan.
Bob's application status: Not approved.
Reason(s):
 The current asset value is insufficient.
 An existing loan prevents approval.
--------

Checking the loan approval status of a person...
[Name: Jack, current asset: 70000, existing loan? False] claims: $30000
Verifying Jack's asset value.
Verifying whether Jack has an existing loan.
Jack's application status: Approved
--------

Checking the loan approval status of a person...
[Name: Tony, current asset: 125000, existing loan? True] claims: $50000
Verifying Tony's asset value.
Verifying whether Tony has an existing loan.
Tony's application status: Not approved.
Reason(s):
 An existing loan prevents approval.
--------
```

Analysis

This demonstration shows that if there is a large number of subsystems, managing those subsystems through a facade can simplify communication.

Let us now review the important points before you move on to the next section:

- You make a simplified interface for your client, and you reduce the number of objects that a client needs to deal with. Notice that the client does not need to create any subsystem instances (e.g., an Asset or ExistingLoanChecker instance) to know the final outcome. Instead, there is a LoanApprover instance that acts as the only point of contact for checking the application status.

- In the future, if there are any new criteria to get a loan, the loan approver can take the responsibility to handle the situation. I believe that you value this point.
- Have you noticed that inside the client code, you do not expose your background verification logic? I believe that you value this point too.

Integrating External APIs

External APIs are often hard to use directly due to differences across platforms. The following demonstration will show how a Facade can provide a **unified interface over heterogeneous external APIs** with different rules and method signatures.

In this demonstration, you'll see three classes—FacebookApi, InstagramApi, and LinkedInApi—that are placed in the Ch04.Facade.External namespace to mimic the scenario where you are about to use services provided by three external APIs. **I assume that these external classes do not share a common interface because their APIs are intentionally designed to be different.** You'll see that each platform exposes methods with platform-specific names and semantics (e.g., publishOnLinkedIn vs. postOnFacebook). Introducing a common interface would require normalizing these differences, which would either reduce clarity or introduce additional patterns such as an Adapter. **To maintain a strict focus on the Facade pattern, this demo preserves the original API differences and allows the Facade to provide a single, unified entry point.**

In addition, while using these platform-specific methods, let us assume the following:

- You cannot post empty messages either using FacebookApi or LinkedInApi, but you can post them using InstagramApi.
- Similar to standard LinkedIn post restrictions, in your application, the LinkedInApi does not allow users to publish a post that exceeds 3000 characters.

POINT TO NOTE

These constraints are intentionally introduced to demonstrate how platform-specific rules can be handled behind a Facade.

Let us investigate the code now. First, see the content of the three classes—FacebookApi, InstagramApi, and LinkedInApi:

// FacebookApi.cs

```
using static System.Console;

namespace Ch04.Facade.External
{
    public class FacebookApi
    {
        public void PostOnFacebook(string message)
        {
            if (string.IsNullOrWhiteSpace(message))
            {
                throw new ArgumentException("Message cannot be empty.");
            }
            WriteLine($"[Facebook]: {message}");
        }
    }
}
```

// LinkedInApi.cs

```
using static System.Console;

namespace Ch04.Facade.External
{
    public class LinkedInApi
    {
        private const int MaxLength = 3000;

        public void PublishOnLinkedIn(string message)
        {
            if (string.IsNullOrWhiteSpace(message))
            {
                throw new ArgumentException("Message cannot be empty.");
            }
            if (message.Length > MaxLength)
            {
```

```
                throw new ArgumentException($"Message exceeds the maximum " +
                    $"allowed length of {MaxLength} characters. " +
                    $"Current length: {message.Length}.");
            }
            WriteLine($"[LinkedIn]: {message}");
        }
    }
}
```

```
// InstagramApi.cs

using static System.Console;

namespace Ch04.Facade.External
{
    public class InstagramApi
    {
        public void PostOnInstagram(string message)
        {
            WriteLine("[Instagram]: " + message);
        }
    }
}
```

To avoid accidental user input, instead of using the string data type, I'd like to use the following enum type in the upcoming demonstration:

```
// Platform.cs

namespace Ch04.Facade.Demo2
{
    public enum Platform
    {
        Facebook,
        LinkedIn,
        Instagram
    }
}
```

Let's see the Facade now:

POINT TO NOTE

In Demonstration 1, the subsystem objects were instantiated **inside a method** of the Facade class (LoanApprover.cs) for simplicity. In contrast, in this demonstration, the Facade class (SocialMediaFacade.cs) instantiates the subsystem classes **in its constructor** as follows:

```
public SocialMediaFacade()
{
   _facebookApi = new FacebookApi();
   _linkedinApi = new LinkedInApi();
   _instagramApi = new InstagramApi();
}
```

Once again, our focus is now on the Facade pattern only. So, this tight coupling is used only for easy readability in this demonstration. In enterprise apps, Dependency Injection is typically used to manage these external service instances. Constructor injection, for example, in this case, could help us achieve loose coupling, easier testing, and better maintainability.

```
// SocialMediaFacade.cs

using Ch04.Facade.External;
using static System.Console;

namespace Ch04.Facade.Demo2
{
   public class SocialMediaFacade
   {
      private readonly FacebookApi _facebookApi;
      private readonly LinkedInApi _linkedinApi;
      private readonly InstagramApi _instagramApi;

      // Architecture Note: This demo uses tight coupling for readability.
      // In enterprise apps, Dependency Injection is typically used to
      // manage these external service instances. For example, in the
```

```
// production environment, you can opt for constructor injection
// to ensure loose coupling and easier testing.

public SocialMediaFacade()
{
    _facebookApi = new FacebookApi();
    _linkedinApi = new LinkedInApi();
    _instagramApi = new InstagramApi();
}
public void Post(string message, params Platform[] platforms)
{
    if (platforms == null || platforms.Length == 0)
    {
        throw new ArgumentException(
            "Select at least one platform to publish the message.");
    }

    foreach (Platform platform in platforms)
    {
        try
        {
            switch (platform)
            {
                case Platform.Facebook:
                    _facebookApi.PostOnFacebook(message);
                    break;
                case Platform.LinkedIn:
                    _linkedinApi.PublishOnLinkedIn(message);
                    break;
                case Platform.Instagram:
                    _instagramApi.PostOnInstagram(message);
                    break;
                default:
                    throw new ArgumentException($"Unexpected value: {platform}");
            }
        }
```

```
                catch (Exception e)
                {
                    WriteLine($"Failed posting on {platform}: {e.Message}");
                }
            } // end foreach
        }
    }
}
```

Demonstration 2

Here is a sample client to test our example:

```
// FacadeDemo2.cs

using static System.Console;

namespace Ch04.Facade.Demo2
{
    public class FacadeDemo2
    {
        public static void Main()
        {
            SocialMediaFacade facade = new();

            // Posting on Facebook
            facade.Post("Hello, friends...",
                Platform.Facebook);
            WriteLine("--------");

            // Posting on Facebook and LinkedIn
            facade.Post("Learning the Facade pattern.",
                Platform.Facebook,
                Platform.LinkedIn);
            WriteLine("--------");

            // Posting on Instagram, LinkedIn, and Facebook
            facade.Post("Hello Everyone...",
                Platform.Instagram,
```

```
                Platform.LinkedIn,
                Platform.Facebook);
            WriteLine("--------");
        }
    }
}
```

Output

The following output confirms that you can successfully post your message on one or more platforms using a facade:

```
[Facebook]: Hello, friends...
--------
[Facebook]: Learning the Facade pattern.
[LinkedIn]: Learning the Facade pattern.
--------
[Instagram]: Hello Everyone...
[LinkedIn]: Hello Everyone...
[Facebook]: Hello Everyone...
--------
```

Q&A Session

Q4.1 What are the key advantages of using the Facade pattern?

Here are some advantages:

- If your system consists of many subsystems, managing those subsystems becomes tough, and clients will find it difficult to communicate separately with each of these subsystems. In a case like this, the Facade pattern is handy. Instead of presenting complex subsystems, you provide a single simplified interface to clients.
- As a result, it reduces the number of objects that a client needs to access.
- This approach also supports loose coupling by separating the client code from the subsystems.

Q4.2 Does the facade class in Demonstration 2 use composition? If so, is this intentional?

Yes. In Demonstration 2, the facade maintains references to the subsystem objects (FacebookApi, LinkedInApi, and InstagramApi) as private fields and delegates work to them. This is a classic example of composition and allows the facade to coordinate multiple subsystems while exposing a simplified interface to the client.

Demonstration 1 follows a slightly different approach. There, the facade creates and uses the subsystem objects (Asset and ExistingLoanChecker) locally inside the CheckLoanEligibility() method. Although those objects are not maintained as fields, the facade still coordinates and delegates work to them rather than relying on inheritance.

More generally, facades typically rely on object collaboration and composition rather than inheritance.

Q4.3 However, it appears to me that you could access each of the subsystems directly. Isn't it?

Your observation is correct. Indeed, the Facade pattern does not restrict you from doing this. But in that case, the code may look messy, and you may lose the benefits associated with the Facade pattern. In this context, note that since the client can directly access the subsystem, it is called a **transparent** facade. But when you restrict that usage and force the client to use the Facade class instance only, it is an **opaque** facade.

Q4.4 How is the Facade pattern different from the Adapter design pattern?

In the Adapter pattern, you try to alter an interface so that your clients do not see the difference between the interfaces. By contrast, the Facade pattern simplifies the interface. So, a client can interact with a simple interface instead of using a complex subsystem.

Q4.5 There should be only one facade for a complex subsystem. Is this correct?

No. You can create multiple facades for a subsystem.

Q4.6 What are the challenges associated with this pattern?

Here are some challenges:

- Subsystems are connected to the Facade layer. So, you need to maintain an additional layer of coding (increasing the codebase).
- As a result, when the internal structure of a subsystem changes, you need to incorporate the changes in the Facade layer as well.

- Developers need to learn about this new layer, whereas some of them may already be familiar with using the subsystems/APIs directly and efficiently.

Q4.7 You have briefly talked about static facade classes in C#. When should I use them? I'd also like to know whether a similar approach can be used in a different programming language, say, Java?

In many examples, there is only one facade, and you may not need to instantiate the facade class. In such cases, it makes sense to make the facade class **static** in C#. However, remember that a static class in C# needs to follow certain language restrictions as well. For example, at the time of this writing, a static class cannot be instantiated, contains only static members, is sealed by default, and cannot contain instance constructors. In fact, a static class in C# is compiled as implicitly abstract and sealed.

In Java, however, you cannot create a top-level static class. The Java Language Specification (Java SE 25) (see https://docs.oracle.com/javase/specs/jls/se25/html/jls-8.html#jls-8.1.1) states that **the modifier static pertains only to member classes and local classes.**

So, while the concept of a static facade is natural in C#, in Java, you can typically simulate this behavior using a class with static methods or by preventing instantiation through other design techniques (e.g., using a private constructor).

Pro Tip: A static class is implicitly abstract and sealed. To examine this, consider the following code:

```
using System;
static class Sample {
}
```

Now you can verify the IL code (to do this quickly, I often use SharpLab.io[1]). Here is a sample IL code for your immediate reference:

```
.class private auto ansi abstract sealed beforefieldinit Sample
   extends [System.Runtime]System.Object
{
}
```

[1] https://sharplab.io/

Summary

The Facade pattern hides complex implementation details by exposing a simple interface and promotes loose coupling between clients and subsystems. This chapter presented two demonstrations to illustrate the pattern. In the first demonstration, the focus was on simplifying the usage of internal subsystems. In the second demonstration, the pattern was applied to provide a unified interface for handling heterogeneous external APIs with different rules and method signatures.

CHAPTER 5

Bridge Pattern

The Bridge pattern is a strong promoter of flexibility and extensibility. Using this pattern, you separate an abstraction from its implementation so that both can evolve independently. Understanding this pattern may appear difficult in the beginning, but once you go through the examples along with the implementations, you'll value the concept behind this pattern.

Concept

The Gang of Four (GoF) defined the intent of this pattern as follows:

> *Decouple an abstraction from its implementation so that the two can vary independently.*

What is the benefit? You can modify different class hierarchies independently without affecting each other. Do not be surprised! Let me explain with an example:

Consider a seller who currently sells televisions both online and offline (at different showrooms). Following the traditional inheritance mechanism, you can design an application for this seller as shown in Figure 5-1.

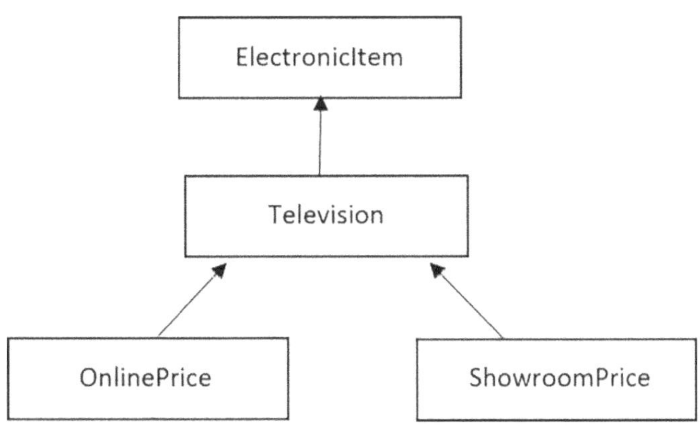

***Figure 5-1.** The Television class inherits from ElectronicItem. The OnlinePrice and ShowroomPrice inherit from the Television class*

V. Sarcar, *The Structural Design Toolkit for C#*, https://doi.org/10.1007/979-8-8688-3029-7_5

If the seller decides to sell mobile phones in the future, you'll probably update the design as shown in Figure 5-2.

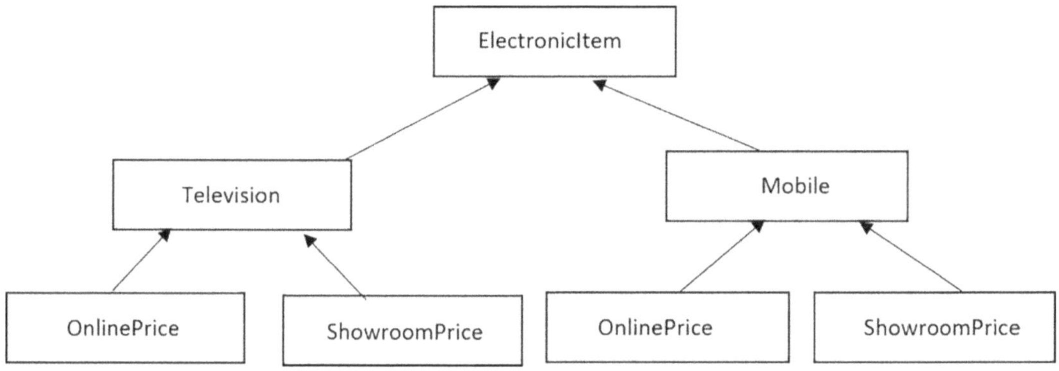

***Figure 5-2.** The Television and Mobile classes inherit from ElectronicItem. Both the Television and Mobile classes have subclasses—OnlinePrice and ShowroomPrice*

You can see that you needed to introduce multiple classes for online and offline mobile sales. It is probably still manageable! However, if you want to include new price schemes by introducing classes such as ThirdPartyPrice or FestiveTimePrice, you'll need to change this design. In addition, if the seller wants to sell new electronic items, like an air conditioner (AC) or a refrigerator, you will again change the design. **You face these challenges because the "electronic item hierarchy" and the corresponding "pricing hierarchy" are tightly coupled in this design.** But in a real-world scenario, this kind of enhancement is often required.

The Bridge pattern addresses this issue! Here, you start with a loosely coupled system for future enhancement. **As a first step, you separate the items from their pricing schemes and place them in separate hierarchies.** As a result, these hierarchies (electronic items and their pricing schemes) can grow independently.

This is why, in the upcoming implementation, you'll see that on one side, the Television class inherits from the abstract class ElectronicItem, and on the other side, the OnlinePrice and ShowroomPrice classes implement the IPricingScheme interface.

Next, you maintain a reference to IPricingScheme inside ElectronicItem to maintain a connection (the bridge) between an item and the corresponding price.

If the seller sells only televisions, after following these steps, you'll end up with the design shown in Figure 5-3.

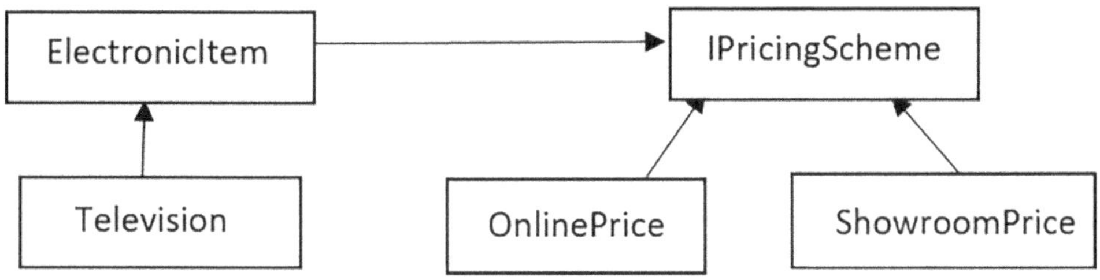

Figure 5-3. *The Television class still inherits from ElectronicItem, but the OnlinePrice and ShowroomPrice classes now implement the IPricingScheme interface. Thus, the Bridge pattern maintains two separate hierarchies*

What is the advantage? If the seller decides to sell mobiles in the near future as well, you can just add one class as shown in Figure 5-4.

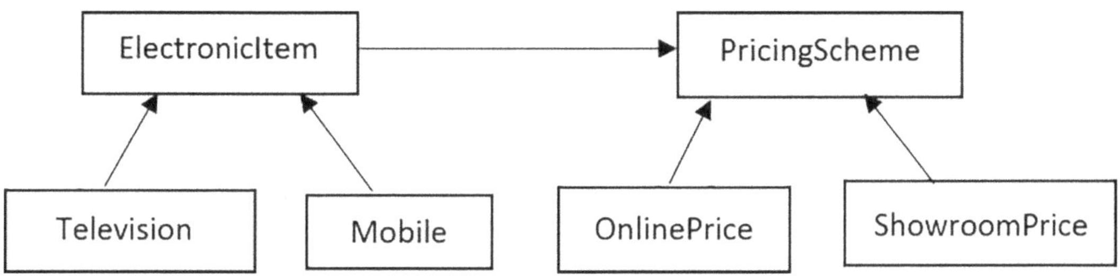

Figure 5-4. *The Mobile class has been added to the ElectronicItem hierarchy, but the PricingScheme hierarchy is unchanged*

You can see that if you had followed the traditional inheritance mechanism, as shown in Figure 5-1, you'd need to consider online and showroom pricing for mobiles as well. **So, to fulfill the criteria, adding a single class would not be sufficient!**

INHERITANCE VERSUS COMPOSITION

In a traditional inheritance tree, adding one new item (like a Mobile or an AC) requires you to create a subclass for every possible pricing scheme. This leads to a **class explosion**. The Bridge pattern solves this by switching from an **"is-a"** relationship to a **"has-a"** relationship (composition).

Real-Life Example

In a software product development company, the development team and the marketing team both play crucial roles. Normally, the marketing team conducts a market survey and gathers customer requirements. The development team implements those requirements in the product to fulfill the customers' needs. Any change (say, in the operational strategy) in one team should not directly impact the other team. This separation allows both teams to evolve independently without tightly coupling their responsibilities.

Let's consider another example: a universal remote control that can work with televisions from different manufacturers. The remote control provides the abstraction (e.g., PowerOn, PowerOff, and ChangeChannel), while each television manufacturer provides its own implementation for carrying out those operations. If a new television brand enters the market, you can add a new implementation without changing the remote-control abstraction. Likewise, if you introduce a more advanced remote control with additional features, you can extend the abstraction without modifying the existing television implementations. This separation allows both hierarchies to evolve independently.

Computer World Example

GUI frameworks can use the Bridge pattern to separate abstractions from platform-specific implementations. For example, using this pattern, you can separate a window abstraction from a window implementation for Linux or macOS.

A similar concept can also be seen in .NET through ADO.NET, where classes such as DbConnection serve as abstractions and provider-specific implementations (e.g., SqlConnection from SQL Server providers or MySqlConnection from MySQL providers) serve as concrete implementors.

Implementation

It's time to see some implementations. While explaining the concept, we considered a seller who currently sells televisions both online and offline (at different showrooms). Let's design an application keeping these things in mind. So, as stated earlier, you'll see two different hierarchies—one for the electronic items and the other for the associated pricing schemes.

Since the pricing hierarchy is very simple, let's begin with this.

POINT TO NOTE

The electronic items and their corresponding pricing schemes are maintained in two separate hierarchies. Following C# naming conventions, I'll place the pricing hierarchy in the Ch05.Bridge.Pricing namespace and the other hierarchy in the Ch05.Bridge.Items namespace.

The Pricing Hierarchy

This hierarchy starts with the following interface:

```
namespace Ch05.Bridge.Pricing
{
  public interface IPricingScheme
  {
    double GetPrice(double printedPrice);
  }

}
```

The OnlinePrice class implements this interface. Notice that the GetPrice method provides a 10% discount for the online purchases:

```
namespace Ch05.Bridge.Pricing
{
  public class OnlinePrice : IPricingScheme
  {
    public double GetPrice(double printedPrice)
    {
      return printedPrice * 0.9; // with 10% discount
    }
  }
}
```

The ShowroomPrice class also implements IPricingScheme. However, the direct purchases from these showrooms do not provide any discount on the printed price:

```
namespace Ch05.Bridge.Pricing
{
    public class ShowroomPrice : IPricingScheme
    {
        public double GetPrice(double printedPrice)
        {
            return printedPrice; // no discount
        }
    }
}
```

The Item Hierarchy

The abstract class ElectronicItem sits at the top of this hierarchy and maintains a reference to IPricingScheme. Let's see it:

```
using Ch05.Bridge.Pricing;

namespace Ch05.Bridge.Items
{
    public abstract class ElectronicItem(IPricingScheme scheme)
    {
        // Composition - implementor
        protected readonly IPricingScheme _scheme = scheme;

        protected abstract double GetPrintedPrice();
        public double GetFinalPrice()
        {
            return _scheme.GetPrice(GetPrintedPrice());
        }
    }
}
```

The Television class extends this class as follows:

```
using Ch05.Bridge.Pricing;

namespace Ch05.Bridge.Items
{
   public class Television(IPricingScheme scheme, double printedPrice)
      : ElectronicItem(scheme)
   {
      private readonly double _printedPrice = printedPrice;
      protected override double GetPrintedPrice()
      {
         return _printedPrice;
      }
   }
}
```

The Mobile class is very similar:

```
using Ch05.Bridge.Pricing;

namespace Ch05.Bridge.Items
{
   public class Mobile(IPricingScheme scheme, double printedPrice)
      : ElectronicItem(scheme)
   {
      private readonly double _printedPrice = printedPrice;
      protected override double GetPrintedPrice()
      {
         return _printedPrice;
      }
   }
}
```

Class Diagram

Before you see the client code, let us verify the design structure using the class diagram shown in Figure 5-5 as well (I have marked the separate hierarchies and pointed out the bridge for your easy reference).

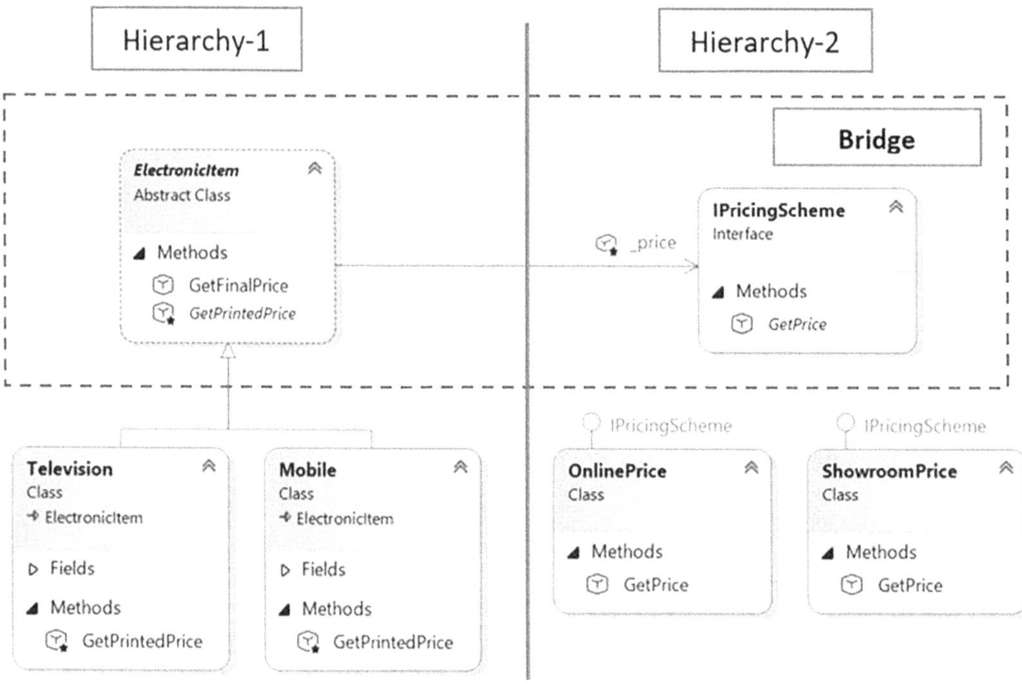

***Figure 5-5.** Key participants of the Demonstration 1*

Demonstration 1

It's time to see a sample client (BridgeDemo1.cs):

```
// BridgeDemo1.cs

using Ch05.Bridge.Items;
using Ch05.Bridge.Pricing;

using static System.Console;
```

```
namespace Ch05.Bridge.Demo1
{
    internal class BridgeDemo1
    {
        static void Main(string[] args)
        {
            WriteLine("***Bridge Pattern Demo.***");

            WriteLine("Verifying the market price of a television " +
                "that has a printed price of $2000.");
            ElectronicItem tvOnline = new Television(new OnlinePrice(), 2000);
            ElectronicItem tvShowroom = new Television(new ShowroomPrice(), 2000);
            WriteLine($"The TV's online price: {tvOnline.GetFinalPrice()}");
            WriteLine($"The TV's showroom price: {tvShowroom.GetFinalPrice()}");

            WriteLine("\nVerifying the market price of a mobile phone " +
                "that has a printed price of $5000.");
            ElectronicItem mobileOnline = new Mobile(new OnlinePrice(), 5000);
            ElectronicItem mobileShowroom = new Mobile(new ShowroomPrice(), 5000);
            WriteLine($"The mobile's online price: {mobileOnline.GetFinalPrice()}");
            WriteLine($"The mobile's showroom price: {mobileShowroom.GetFinalPrice()}");
        }
    }
}
```

Output

Here's the output:

```
***Bridge Pattern Demo.***
Verifying the market price of a television that has a printed price of $2000.
The TV's online price: $1800
The TV's showroom price: $2000

Verifying the market price of a mobile phone that has a printed price of $5000.
The mobile's online price: $4500
The mobile's showroom price: $5000
```

Refined Abstraction

Demonstration 1 helped you avoid a "class explosion" by separating items from their pricing schemes. However, you might wonder: **"Does this pattern limit us to only the common behavior defined in the base abstraction?"** The answer is **no. In fact, in real systems, certain products often require specialized behavior without justifying an entirely new abstraction hierarchy.**

To illustrate, the following demonstration focuses on a **refined abstraction**. Let's assume the seller would like to offer a special promotional discount on mobiles but not on televisions. To fulfill this requirement, you can add a specific method (shown in bold) to the Mobile class as follows:

```
using Ch05.Bridge.Pricing;

namespace Ch05.Bridge.Items
{
  public class Mobile(IPricingScheme scheme, double printedPrice)
    : ElectronicItem(scheme)
  {
    private readonly double _printedPrice = printedPrice;
    protected override double GetPrintedPrice()
    {
      return _printedPrice;
    }
    #region This specific method is added for Demonstration 2
    // This method is added to provide a special promotional discount
    public double GetFestiveTimePrice(double discountPercent)
    {
      double priceBeforeDiscount = GetFinalPrice();
      return priceBeforeDiscount * (1 - discountPercent / 100);
    }
    #endregion
  }
}
```

POINT TO NOTE

In the previous code segment, the priceBeforeDiscount variable is used to store the price value before applying the promotional discount. For example, if the printed price of a mobile is $5000, the online price before applying the promotional discount would be $4500, and the showroom price would be $5000 (since there is no discount). However, if the 20% promotional discount is further applied, the online and showroom prices of this mobile would be $3600 and $4000, respectively.

However, depending on business requirements, any special discount could be applied before or after the pricing scheme. Both approaches are valid and illustrate different business semantics.

Demonstration 2

Let's test this enhancement using the following sample class:

```
using Ch05.Bridge.Items;
using Ch05.Bridge.Pricing;

using static System.Console;

namespace Ch05.Bridge.Demo2
{
    internal class BridgeDemo2
    {
        static void Main(string[] args)
        {
            WriteLine("***Bridge Pattern Demonstration-2 ***");

            WriteLine("Verifying the market price of a television " +
                "that has a printed price of $2000.");
            ElectronicItem tvOnline = new Television(new OnlinePrice(), 2000);
            ElectronicItem tvShowroom = new Television(new ShowroomPrice(), 2000);
            WriteLine($"The TV's online price: {tvOnline.GetFinalPrice()}");
            WriteLine($"The TV's showroom price: {tvShowroom.GetFinalPrice()}");
```

```
            WriteLine("\nVerifying the market price of a mobile phone " +
              "that has a printed price of $5000.");
            ElectronicItem mobileOnline = new Mobile(new OnlinePrice(), 5000);
            ElectronicItem mobileShowroom = new Mobile(new ShowroomPrice(), 5000);
            WriteLine($"The mobile's online price: {mobileOnline.GetFinalPrice()}");
            WriteLine($"The mobile's showroom price: {mobileShowroom.GetFinalPrice()}");

            // Testing Demo-2 enhancements here
            WriteLine("\nVerifying 'Promotional discounts' on the market price " +
              "of a mobile phone that has a printed price of $5000.");
            WriteLine($"The mobile's online price: {((Mobile)mobileOnline).GetFestiveTimePrice(20)}");
            WriteLine($"The mobile's showroom price: {((Mobile)mobileShowroom).GetFestiveTimePrice(20)}");
        }
    }
}
```

Output

Here is the new output with the changes in bold:

```
***Bridge Pattern Demonstration-2 ***
Verifying the market price of a television that has a printed price of $2000.
The TV's online price: $1800
The TV's showroom price: $2000

Verifying the market price of a mobile phone that has a printed price of $5000.
The mobile's online price: $4500
The mobile's showroom price: $5000

Verifying 'Promotional discounts' on the market price of a mobile phone that has a printed price of $5000.
The mobile's online price: $3600
The mobile's showroom price: $4000
```

Analysis

You can see that the seller gave an additional 20% discount when mobiles are sold during the promotional period. This demonstration illustrated two critical points:

- **Independent Variation:** You can add specialized logic to a specific abstraction without changing the ElectronicItem base class or any of the IPricingScheme implementations.
- **Refined Abstraction Behavior:** You saw how a refined abstraction (mobile) can introduce product-specific logic (e.g., a variable discount—20% in this example) without affecting other abstractions.

Now you can see that the Bridge pattern is not just a way to organize code, but a flexible architecture that supports complex, overlapping business requirements.

Q&A Session

Q5.1 What are the key advantages of using a Bridge design pattern?

In this chapter, I showed two examples to demonstrate that you can avoid tight coupling between items and their corresponding prices by maintaining two separate hierarchies, both of which can be extended without affecting the other. In programming terms, you can vary the abstraction and the implementation hierarchies independently.

Q5.2 "You could use simple subclassing instead of using this kind of design."—Is this correct?

No. With simple subclassing, your implementations cannot vary dynamically. Your implementations may seem to behave differently, but actually, they are bound to the abstraction at compile time.

You have also seen that traditional inheritance can cause **class explosions.** (While discussing the concept of this pattern, do you remember that adding one new item [like a mobile or an AC] to an existing architecture required us to create subclasses for every possible pricing scheme?) The Bridge pattern solves this by switching from an **"is-a"** relationship to a **"has-a"** relationship (composition).

Q5.3 What are the challenges associated with this pattern?

Here are some challenges:

- The overall structure is relatively complex.
- Here, you do not directly invoke a method. Instead, the abstraction layer delegates the work to the implementation layer. So, you may notice a slight performance impact when you execute an operation.

Q5.4 I see some similarities between a bridge design pattern and an adapter design pattern. Am I right?

Indeed, the bridge pattern is often confused with the adapter pattern, most commonly with an object adapter design pattern. Since both patterns rely on **object composition** and **delegation**, this confusion is natural. These are only surface-level similarities. However, the **intent, timing, and design goals** of the Bridge and Adapter patterns differ fundamentally.

The Bridge pattern is a **proactive design choice**. When designing a system, you typically apply this pattern to prevent tight coupling by separating an abstraction from its implementation, allowing both to **evolve independently**. For example, in this chapter, the separation between the ElectronicItem hierarchy and the PricingScheme hierarchy was deliberate, and this was planned **from the beginning**. Both hierarchies are designed together, with the expectation that new items and new pricing strategies will be introduced over time.

In contrast, the Adapter pattern is typically a **reactive solution**. It is often introduced to integrate existing components that were not originally designed to work together. **You introduce an adapter when you want to reuse existing code but discover that its interface is incompatible with what your client expects—and you cannot (or should not) modify that existing code.** An adapter, therefore, acts as a wrapper that translates one interface into another (often referred to as "making two existing things work together").

To relate this distinction directly to the examples in this chapter, let's examine the following points:

- ElectronicItem is **not adapting an existing pricing API**. Both sides are designed to collaborate **from the start**, with clearly defined roles.

- In addition, IPricingScheme is not an existing or third-party interface being adapted. It is **explicitly designed to be used by ElectronicItem**, and no translation or interface conversion is required.
- The pricing logic is meant to **vary independently**, not merely be "made compatible."

POINT TO NOTE

In the Bridge pattern, delegation is part of the core abstraction's responsibility. In the Adapter pattern, delegation exists only to hide incompatibility from the client. So, you can consider Bridge as a **proactive** design choice while Adapter as a **reactive** fix.

In short, while both patterns use composition, **Bridge is about planned decoupling, whereas Adapter is about retrospective compatibility** (i.e., you add compatibility after the original design is completed). This is why understanding the intent behind the design—not just the class structure—is the key to distinguishing between them.

Q5.5 Do I need to maintain a one-to-one mapping between an abstraction class method and an implementor method?

No. A single method in the abstraction can use **multiple methods** from the implementor.

To illustrate, let us add a **default implementation** (available since C# 8.0, which is supported in .NET Core 3.0 and later[1]) inside the IPricingScheme interface as follows:

```
using static System.Console;

namespace Ch05.Bridge.Pricing
{
  public interface IPricingScheme
  {
    double GetPrice(double printedPrice);
```

[1] https://learn.microsoft.com/en-us/dotnet/csharp/whats-new/csharp-version-history

```
        #region The following method is added for Q5.5
        void ConveyThanks()
        {
            WriteLine("Thank you for being interested in the product.");
        }
        #endregion
    }
}
```

Now you can use this method in the GetFinalPrice() of the ElectronicItem class as follows (shown in bold):

```
using Ch05.Bridge.Pricing;

namespace Ch05.Bridge.Items
{
    public abstract class ElectronicItem(IPricingScheme scheme)
    {
        // Composition - implementor
        protected readonly IPricingScheme _scheme = scheme;

        protected abstract double GetPrintedPrice();
        public double GetFinalPrice()
        {
            // The following line is added for Q5.5
            _scheme.ConveyThanks();
            return _scheme.GetPrice(GetPrintedPrice());
        }
    }
}
```

Notice the GetFinalPrice() method. It now uses multiple methods—ConveyThanks() and GetPrice(...)—from the IPricingScheme hierarchy. This shows that a high-level abstraction method can delegate work to **multiple implementor methods**, while the clients remain unaware of these internal interactions.

Before I conclude the chapter, let me tell you that these changes modify the output of Demonstration 1 as follows:

```
***Bridge Pattern Demo.***
Verifying the market price of a television that has a printed price of $2000.
Thank you for being interested in the product.
The TV's online price: $1800
Thank you for being interested in the product.
The TV's showroom price: $2000

Verifying the market price of a mobile phone that has a printed price of $5000.
Thank you for being interested in the product.
The mobile's online price: $4500
Thank you for being interested in the product.
The mobile's showroom price: $5000
```

Summary

In this chapter, you learned how the Bridge pattern decouples an abstraction from its implementation so that both can evolve independently. By separating electronic items from their pricing schemes, you avoided tight coupling and the resulting class explosion commonly seen in inheritance-based designs.

Through **Demonstration 1**, you saw how composition enables flexible combinations of items and pricing strategies at runtime. **Demonstration 2** extended this idea further by focusing on a *refined abstraction*, showing that specialized behavior can be added to a specific abstraction without modifying the base class or the implementation hierarchy.

Overall, this chapter demonstrated that the Bridge pattern is more than just a refactoring technique; it is a powerful architectural approach. It enables you to build extensible, maintainable systems that can handle complex and evolving business requirements with ease.

CHAPTER 6

Composite Pattern

The Composite pattern relies on object composition to model part–whole relationships and allows clients to work with both individual objects and object compositions consistently. This chapter explains this pattern through simple examples.

Concept

The Gang of Four (GoF) defined the intent of the Composite pattern as follows:

> Compose objects into tree structures to represent part-whole hierarchies. Composite lets clients treat individual objects and compositions of objects uniformly.

In object-oriented programming, a composite is an object composed of one or more objects that implement a common interface. Since these objects share the same type and behavioral contract, you can treat them uniformly.

What is the benefit of treating both the composite objects (branches) and the individual objects (leaf nodes) uniformly? It simplifies client code by eliminating conditional logic that distinguishes between simple and composite objects, making the application flexible and less error-prone. The following examples will make the concept clearer.

Real-Life Example

Consider a stationery shop that sells individual items such as pens and pencils. Let's assume that customers can purchase these items individually or as a gift box that contains a combination of pens and pencils. Assume that there is no discount for purchasing multiple items or gift boxes (other than receiving the box itself); therefore, the price of a gift box is the sum of the prices of the individual items it contains.

V. Sarcar, *The Structural Design Toolkit for C#*, https://doi.org/10.1007/979-8-8688-3029-7_6

From the client's perspective, there is no need to distinguish between a single item and a gift box—both represent purchasable items and are processed uniformly. **The Composite pattern is well-suited for such scenarios, where individual objects and compositions of objects must be treated uniformly.**

You can also think of an organization that consists of many departments. In general, an organization typically has many employees. Some of these employees are grouped to form a department, and those departments can be further grouped to build the final structure of the organization.

Computer World Example

This pattern is common in various UI frameworks where you need to add UI controls, such as buttons or text boxes, to a container. In C#, frameworks such as Windows Forms (WinForms) and Windows Presentation Foundation (WPF) provide natural examples of this pattern.

Here are some more examples for you:

- I already mentioned that a tree data structure can follow this concept, where the clients can treat the leaves and non-leaves (or branches) of the tree in the same way. So, when you see hierarchical data, you can get a clue that the Composite pattern can be useful. XML documents and file systems are classic examples of these tree structures.
- In WinForms, UI controls also follow a hierarchical structure that reflects the Composite pattern.

WINFORMS CONTROL HIERARCHY

In Windows Forms, the Control class is the base class for most UI elements. Classes such as Button and TextBox derive from Control and act as leaf nodes, while classes such as Panel and Form also derive from Control but can contain child controls, forming a hierarchical structure. The following code segment shows a typical usage for your immediate reference:

```
Panel panel = new Panel();
panel.Controls.Add(new Button());
```

Implementation

As discussed earlier in the real-life example, consider a shop from which you can purchase pens, pencils, or gift packs of pens and pencils. Let us also assume that these pens and pencils can be either "**black and white (BW)**" or "**colored.**" This is why you'll see the following enum named Color:

// Color.cs

```
namespace Ch06.Composite.Demo1
{
    public enum Color
    {
        Colored,
        BlackAndWhite
    }
}
```

The Common Interface

Each item in our example (a pen or a pencil) has an associated price. So, let me introduce the following interface that contains a Price property as follows:

// IItem.cs

```
namespace Ch06.Composite.Demo1
{
    public interface IItem
    {
        decimal Price { get; }
    }
}
```

Author's Note: This example uses decimal because it focuses on monetary calculations. Some earlier demonstrations used double for simplicity, since the primary goal there was to illustrate a design pattern rather than financial precision. In practice, both types have valid use cases, and the choice depends on the requirements of the application.

The Leaf Classes

The Pen class implements this interface as follows:

// Pen.cs

```
namespace Ch06.Composite.Demo1
{
   public class Pen(Color color) : IItem
   {
      private readonly Color _color = color;
      public decimal Price
      {
         get { return _color == Color.BlackAndWhite ? 15m : 30m; }
      }
   }
}
```

The Pencil class is very similar, except the prices are lower compared to the pens:

// Pencil.cs

```
namespace Ch06.Composite.Demo1
{
   public class Pencil(Color color) : IItem
   {
      private readonly Color _color = color;
      public decimal Price
      {
         get { return _color == Color.BlackAndWhite ? 2.5m : 10m; }
      }
   }
}
```

The Composite Class

GiftPack is the composite class in our example. Here are two important characteristics:

- It implements IItem, so it can be treated like any other single product.
- It maintains a collection of IItem objects, allowing it to store pens, pencils, or even other gift packs.

Keeping these points in mind, consider the following class:

// GiftPack.cs

```
namespace Ch06.Composite.Demo1
{
   public class GiftPack : IItem
   {
      private readonly List<IItem> _items = [];

      // The previous line of code is equivalent to:
      // private readonly List<IItem> _items = new();

      // Flexibility: Add any Item (Pen, Pencil, or another GiftPack)
      public void Add(IItem item)
      {
         _items.Add(item);
      }

      // Remove an item, if needed
      public void Remove(IItem item)
      {
         _items.Remove(item);
      }
      public decimal Price
      {
         get
         {
            decimal totalPrice = 0;
            foreach (IItem item in _items)
            {
               totalPrice += item.Price;
```

```
            }
            return totalPrice;
        }
    }
  }
}
```

Class Diagram

Before you see the client code, let's verify the key structure of our application using the class diagram shown in Figure 6-1.

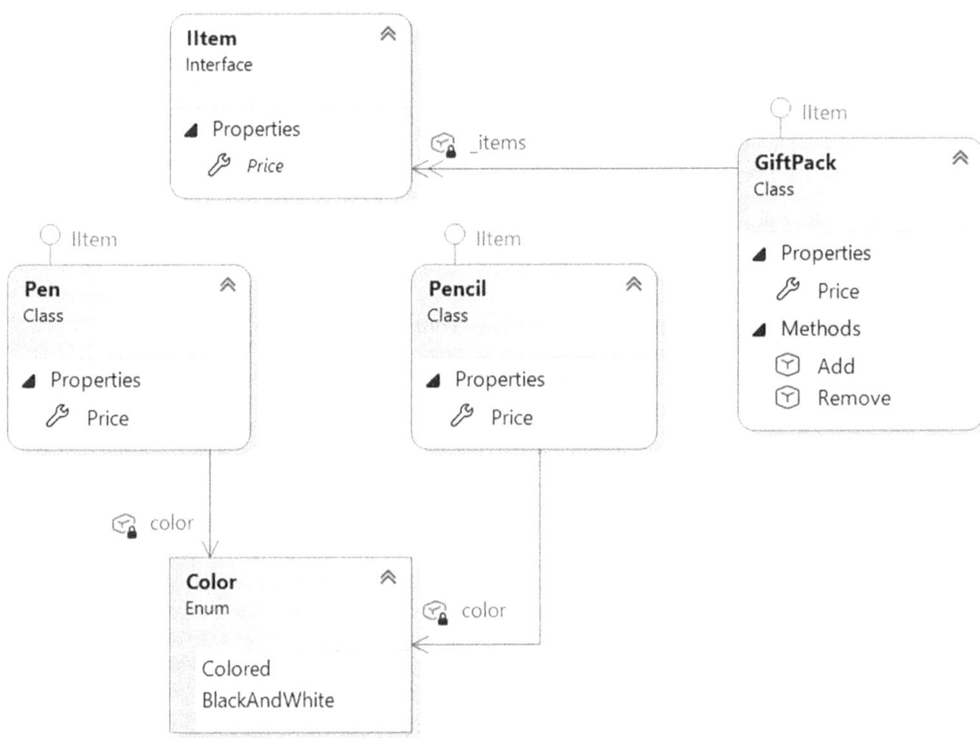

***Figure 6-1.** The structure of the Composite design pattern in Demonstration 1*

Author's Note: The diagram in Figure 6-1 is generated using the Visual Studio Class Designer. Note that the **double arrow (<<)** pointing from GiftPack to IItem represents a **Collection Association** (in this case, a List<IItem>). While standard UML often uses a filled diamond to denote composition relationships, the Class Designer uses this arrow notation to indicate that the composite object maintains a collection of its components.

In addition, the Color type is also shown as an Enum and is referenced only by the leaf classes (Pen and Pencil) as a supporting value type; it does not participate in the Composite structure. It is shown only for clarity in the upcoming implementation.

Demonstration 1

Let's see a sample client code now:

POINT TO NOTE

In Demonstration 2, I'll show you a WinForms application. In WinForms-based applications, names such as Pen and Color may conflict with existing framework types from namespaces such as System.Drawing when both namespaces are visible in the same scope. Therefore, alias directives are shown for the custom types from the Ch06.Composite.Demo1 namespace. The alias for Pencil is optional and is included only to maintain consistency.

```
// CompositeDemo1.cs

using Ch06.Composite.Demo1;
using static System.Console;

// The following aliases may be needed in WinForms demonstrations
// to avoid conflicts with framework types such as Pen and Color.
using Pen = Ch06.Composite.Demo1.Pen;
using Color = Ch06.Composite.Demo1.Color;

// The following line is optional,
// as there is no conflict with Pencil
using Pencil = Ch06.Composite.Demo1.Pencil;

namespace Ch06.Composite.Demo1
{
  class CompositeDemo1
  {
    static void Main()
    {
      IItem pen = new Pen(Color.BlackAndWhite);
      WriteLine($"The BW pen's cost is ${pen.Price}");
```

```
            pen = new Pen(Color.Colored);
            WriteLine($"The colored pen's cost is ${pen.Price}");
            WriteLine("----------------");

            IItem pencil = new Pencil(Color.BlackAndWhite);
            WriteLine($"The BW pencil's cost is ${pencil.Price}");

            pencil = new Pencil(Color.Colored);
            WriteLine($"The colored pencil's cost is ${pencil.Price}");
            WriteLine("----------------");

            GiftPack bwGiftPack = new();
            bwGiftPack.Add(new Pen(Color.BlackAndWhite));
            bwGiftPack.Add(new Pencil(Color.BlackAndWhite));
            WriteLine($"A gift pack with a BW pen and " +
              $"a BW pencil costs ${bwGiftPack.Price}");
            WriteLine("----------------");

            GiftPack bigGiftPack = new();
            bigGiftPack.Add(bwGiftPack); // Adding a composite to a composite
            bigGiftPack.Add(new Pen(Color.Colored));
            bigGiftPack.Add(new Pencil(Color.Colored));
            WriteLine("A gift pack with a BW gift pack, a colored pen, and " +
              $"a colored pencil costs ${bigGiftPack.Price}");
        }
    }
}
```

Output

Here's the output:

```
The BW pen's cost is $15
The colored pen's cost is $30
----------------
The BW pencil's cost is $2.5
The colored pencil's cost is $10
```

```
----------------
A gift pack with a BW pen and a BW pencil costs $17.5
----------------
A gift pack with a BW gift pack, a colored pen, and a colored pencil costs $57.5
```

Q&A Session

Q6.1 In the composite class (GiftPack.cs), you used a list data structure. Can I use another data structure?

Yes, you are free to use any data structure that can efficiently serve your needs. The GoF also confirmed that it is not necessary to use a specific data structure.

Q6.2 In Demonstration 1, the Composite class GiftPack.cs **contains the** Add(IItem item) **and** Remove(IItem item) **methods. Was this intentional?**

There are two variations of the Composite design pattern: one focuses on safety and the other on transparency. This example primarily focuses on safety (often called the safe Composite approach). Since **these operations are meaningless for leaf objects** (the instances of the Pen and Pencil classes), in this variant, only the composite class (GiftPack) exposes these behaviors. As a result, the leaf objects expose only the behavior that is common to all items—the Price property.

You could argue that declaring these Add() and Rem'ove() operations in the IItem interface (**e.g., as default methods**) would allow client code to handle leaf and composite objects uniformly. However, **since leaf objects cannot logically contain children**, such methods would either **remain unused or throw runtime exceptions**, which **reduces type safety** and **may confuse readers.**

By restricting structural operations to the composite class, this design keeps the intent of the Composite pattern clear, ensures compile-time safety, and prevents misuse of leaf objects.

Author's Note: The GoF also mentioned that this kind of decision involves a trade-off between safety and transparency.

Built-In Composites

In this demonstration, we will revisit the Composite pattern using built-in UI components available in C#. **The primary goal is to show how frameworks such as Windows Forms naturally implement the Composite structure, allowing you to work with individual controls and composite containers uniformly, while keeping the example minimal and focused on the core concept.**

Author's Note: Windows Forms is supported only on Windows. However, the Composite structure shown here is not limited to this platform. Cross-platform UI frameworks such as .NET MAUI also organize UI elements in hierarchical UI trees, where layout containers (such as Grid) act as composites and individual controls (such as Button and Label) act as leaf nodes.

Demonstration 2

The upcoming example is similar to the previous example, but uses built-in composites in C#. Here, you'll see the following roles:

- Instances of Button and Label act as leaf objects.
- TableLayoutPanel acts as a composite object that contains leaf objects.
- Form acts as another composite object that contains a TableLayoutPanel.

Author's Note: Form acts as the top-level composite object and contains child controls through its Controls collection. This is conceptually similar to the List<IItem> used inside the GiftPack class in Demonstration 1, where a composite maintains its child components.

In the upcoming implementation, you'll see the following code:

```
// Handling the FormClosing event to close the window
FormClosing += (sender, e) =>
{
  // Additional logic can be placed here if needed

 };
```

Here, the lambda expression is used to handle the FormClosing event. The event expects a delegate with a specific signature (object sender, FormClosingEventArgs e). Instead of defining a separate method, you can provide a concise inline handler using a lambda expression, allowing you to write only the event-handling logic.

I have kept the supporting comments for your easy reference:

POINT TO NOTE

In this example, the TableLayoutPanel is used for layout purposes only. It divides the available space into rows and columns and assigns each control to a specific cell. When docking is set to DockStyle.Fill, each control occupies the full area of its assigned cell. Consequently, controls such as buttons may appear larger than their preferred size. This behavior is due to the layout container and is independent of the Composite pattern.

In the previous demonstrations, the client code was placed in a file such as **<PatternName><DemonstrationNumber>.cs** (e.g., CompositeDemo1.cs in this chapter), similar to other console-based examples in this book. However, this example uses a Windows Forms application, where the entry point is conventionally defined in a Program.cs file. This file initializes the application and launches the main form (CompositeDemo2Form in the upcoming example), which acts as the client in this demonstration.

```
// CompositeDemo2Form.cs

namespace Ch06.Composite.Demo2
{
  public partial class CompositeDemo2Form : Form
  {
    public CompositeDemo2Form()
    {
      InitializeComponent();
      Text = "Composite Pattern Demo-2";
      Width = 300;
      Height = 200;

      // Leaf objects
      Control button = new Button()
```

```
            {
                Text = "Button (Sample)",
                Dock = DockStyle.Fill
            };

            Control label = new Label()
            {
                Text = "Testing built-in composites",
                AutoSize = true,
                Dock = DockStyle.Fill
            };

            // Composite object
            var layout = new TableLayoutPanel()
            {
                RowCount = 2,
                ColumnCount = 1,
                Dock = DockStyle.Fill
            };

            layout.Controls.Add(label, 0, 0);
            layout.Controls.Add(button, 0, 1);

            // Top-level composite
            Controls.Add(layout);

            // Handling the FormClosing event to close the window
            FormClosing += (sender, e) =>
            {
                // Additional logic can be placed here if needed
            };
        }
    }
}
```

// Program.cs

```
namespace Ch06.Composite.Demo2
{
```

```
    internal static class Program
    {
        /// <summary>
        ///  The main entry point for the application.
        /// </summary>
        [STAThread]
        static void Main()
        {
            // To customize application configuration such as
            // set high DPI settings or default font,
            // see https://aka.ms/applicationconfiguration.
            ApplicationConfiguration.Initialize();
            Application.Run(new CompositeDemo2Form());
        }
    }
}
```

Output

Upon running this program, you can see the output shown in Figure 6-2.

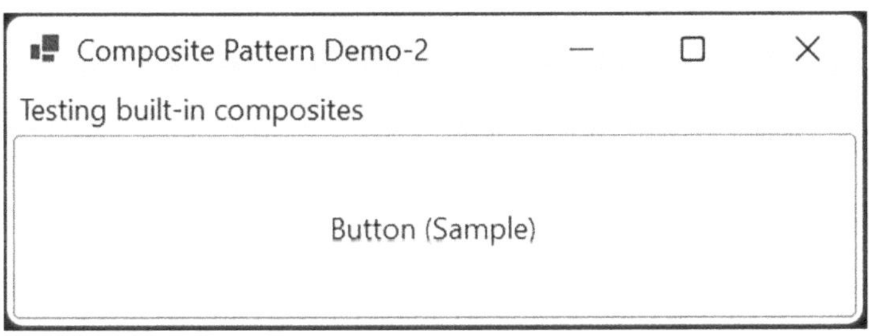

Figure 6-2. *Exercising the built-in composites in C# components*

Author's Note: If you are already familiar with the Iterator pattern, you may notice that in the Price property of the GiftPack class (Demonstration 1), the foreach loop internally relies on C#'s enumeration infrastructure (IEnumerable / IEnumerator). This illustrates how the Composite pattern is often used together with iteration to traverse child components without exposing the underlying data structure. Since this book does not explicitly cover the Iterator pattern, this interaction was not discussed earlier.

Q&A Session

Q6.3 What are the advantages of using the Composite design pattern?

Here are some advantages:

- In a tree-like structure, you can treat both the composite objects (branch nodes) and the individual objects (leaf nodes) uniformly. Notice that in Demonstration 1, I have used the Price property to return the price of an individual item (a pen or pencil) or a composite item (a gift pack).
- It is common to implement a part-whole hierarchy using this design pattern.
- You can easily add a new component to the architecture or delete an existing component from the architecture.

Q6.4 What are the challenges associated with using the Composite design pattern?

Here are some challenges:

- If the order of child components is significant (e.g., in parse trees representing mathematical expressions), additional care may be required to preserve that ordering. For example, **(1 + 2) × 3** produces a different result from **1 + (2 × 3)**. Therefore, rearranging child nodes may change the meaning of the composite structure.
- If you are dealing with immutable objects, you cannot simply delete them.
- If you keep adding new nodes, maintenance can become difficult over time (especially in deeply nested hierarchies). Sometimes you may want to deal with a composite that has special components. This kind of constraint may increase development costs because you may need to implement a dynamic checking mechanism to support the concept.

Q6.5 I have read your other book, *The Structural Design Toolkit for Java*.[1] In a similar context, you used Java AWT. There, you used similar components, such as a button, a label, and a panel, to produce an output similar to Demonstration 2. Also, to close the application, you wrote the following:

```
// Using WindowListener to close the window
    frame.addWindowListener(new WindowAdapter() {
      public void windowClosing(WindowEvent e) {
        // Release resources
        frame.dispose();
        // Trigger shutdown
        System.exit(0);
      }
    });
```

Then you mentioned that the application combines the Composite and Adapter patterns. Does Demonstration 2 **of this chapter also use the Adapter pattern?**

No, Demonstration 2 focuses on the Composite pattern. In Java AWT, examples often use adapter classes such as WindowAdapter. However, WinForms uses delegates and events instead of listener interfaces. Here, you typically subscribe to events (such as Click or FormClosing) by attaching event handlers. This approach differs from Java AWT, where listener interfaces and adapter classes are commonly used.

Therefore, the Adapter pattern is not explicitly demonstrated here, even though similar functionality (handling events) is achieved through a different mechanism.

Q6.6 The FormClosing event in CompositeDemo2Form.cs (Demonstration 2) **seems unnecessary. Is it really needed?**

Not necessarily. In this example, the FormClosing event was introduced to demonstrate how to attach an event handler using a lambda expression. This structure allows you to add custom logic when the form is about to close, which is a common practice in WinForms applications.

To illustrate, consider the following example:

```
FormClosing += (sender, e) =>
{
  #region The following code is added to answer Q6.6
```

[1] https://www.amazon.com/dp/B0GMKZD9NY

```
    var result = MessageBox.Show(
     "Are you sure you want to close?",
      "Confirm",
       MessageBoxButtons.YesNo,
       MessageBoxIcon.Question
    );
    if (result == DialogResult.No)
    {
       e.Cancel = true;
    }
    #endregion
};
```

Now, if you attempt to close the output window, you must confirm your intention by pressing the **Yes** button in the dialog box as shown in Figure 6-3.

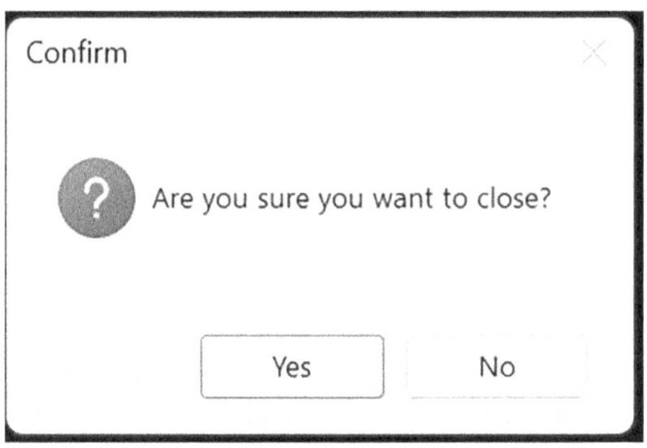

Figure 6-3. *Confirm to close the application*

Summary

The Composite pattern relies on object composition to model part-whole relationships and allows clients to treat individual objects and compositions of objects uniformly. This chapter illustrated the pattern through two implementations. The first one focused exclusively on the Composite pattern and its core usage. The next one demonstrated how built-in UI components in C# (WinForms) naturally realize the Composite structure in practice.

PART II

The Master Workshop—Putting the Toolkit to Work

Part I of the book helped you become familiar with six essential design patterns. **Part II** will help you solidify your understanding by tying all that knowledge together into a single project or mini-application.

This hands-on workshop is designed to show you how multiple structural design patterns can collaborate within a single system to solve real-world design challenges. Rather than studying patterns in isolation, you will see how they interact, complement one another, and address different aspects of a problem simultaneously.

By the end of this part, you will have a clear understanding of how these patterns contribute to building systems that are flexible, maintainable, and scalable.

CHAPTER 7

Building a Report Generation System

Welcome to the project! Let's build a report generation system that demonstrates how multiple design patterns can work together.

Considerations

Before you build the application, you must ensure that you meet the project's requirements. So, let me propose the following requirements for this project:

- **Requirement-1:** A report may consist of multiple elements—such as sections and text blocks.
- **Requirement-2**: The report should be flexible enough to support different output formats, like Console or HTML, without changing the core document structure.
- **Requirement-3:** The system may need to be enhanced in the future with some optional features, such as formatting, logging, or validation, without modifying the core structure.
- **Requirement-4:** Some parts of the system may rely on existing or legacy components, and certain operations (such as loading large sections) should be performed only when required.
- **Requirement-5:** A unified interface should be provided to simplify client usage and hide the internal complexity of the system.

Can you build such an application?

V. Sarcar, *The Structural Design Toolkit for C#*, https://doi.org/10.1007/979-8-8688-3029-7_7

The Architectural Foundation

Let's focus on a sample implementation. To build a truly flexible system, we must start with a solid foundation. The first two requirements give us a clue that we need to handle the following challenges:

- **Structural Complexity:** How do we represent a document that can have multiple levels of nesting (sections within sections)? The Composite pattern can help address this challenge.
- **Output Coupling:** How do we ensure that the document logic isn't "tightly coupled" to a specific output like the Console or a Web Browser? The Bridge pattern can be used to address this issue.

Key Takeaway

The Composite pattern defines **what the document looks like structurally**, while the Bridge pattern defines **how that structure is rendered**. By **combining these patterns**, we can address both challenges effectively.

POINT TO NOTE

I have placed all the code for this project in Ch07.ReportEngine namespace. I won't show this repeatedly while discussing the upcoming code segments. In addition, while implementing the project, I have used the following statement: **using static System.Console;** at the beginning of the file. Therefore, you'll see **WriteLine(...)** instead of **Console.WriteLine(...)** in the upcoming code segments.

Defining Contracts

The next question is: how can these patterns work together? You guessed it right! As a first step, we can establish meaningful contracts. Let's focus on the Composite contract first.

The Composite Contract

By defining the IDocumentComponent interface, we establish a common contract for all document elements while keeping them decoupled from specific rendering implementations. So, here is the first contract that helps implement the Composite pattern:

```
// === COMPOSITE CONTRACT ===

public interface IDocumentComponent
{
  void Render(IRenderer renderer);
}
```

Author's Note: We'll discuss IRenderer shortly.

DESIGN NOTE

You might wonder why we chose the method name Render(…) instead of something like Print(…) or Format(…). In professional C# development, **rendering** often represents the entire pipeline—from interpreting the structural hierarchy (Composite) to applying dynamic styles (Decorator) and finally outputting to a specific medium (Bridge). It indicates that our engine is doing more than just printing; it is transforming a logical document model into a rendered representation (i.e., into a visual reality).

Styling

Before we can render anything, we need a way to communicate **styling intent**. To make things simple, you can use an enum called TextStyle as follows:

```
public enum TextStyle
{
   Bold,
   Italic,
}
```

DESIGN NOTE

In this design, styles are not stored inside the document nodes themselves. Instead, they are communicated during rendering and interpreted differently depending on the selected renderer.

This separation is intentional—it allows the same document model to produce different visual outputs without structural changes. In short, the Composite structure remains completely unaware of styling.

You may also note that we have not defined something like BoldAndItalic or ItalicAndBold. Why? We aim to build a scalable application in which styles can be composed easily using the Decorator pattern, rather than adding more enum values. Therefore, in this design, styles remain independent and are applied sequentially. This approach allows different renderers to interpret their combination in different ways.

The Bridge Contracts

It's time to focus on the Bridge contracts. At this stage, we are defining a **minimal contract** that is sufficient to support our current requirements—rendering text and applying simple styles.

DESIGN NOTE

In real-world systems, this interface can evolve over time as new requirements emerge (e.g., handling images, tables, or advanced formatting). However, starting with a small and focused contract keeps the design simple; that is, it'll be easier to understand.

These are as follows:

```
// === BRIDGE CONTRACTS ===

public interface IRenderer
{
    void RenderText(string text);
    void StartStyle(TextStyle style);
    void EndStyle(TextStyle style);
}
```

Implementing Contracts

It's time to implement the contracts that we defined earlier. Let's begin implementing the composite contract.

Implementing the Composite Contract

Both the Text and Section classes implement the IDocumentComponent interface. **Why are there two classes?** Easy guess—the instances of the Text class will act as the **leaf** nodes, and the instances of the Section class will act as the **composite** nodes.

You may note that the Section class doesn't contain any rendering logic—it delegates the rendering responsibility to its children by iterating over them and passing the renderer along.

REMINDER

I have used primary constructors in the following code segment. You know that this is a modern C# feature. I have also simplified the collection initialization. This feature was introduced in C# 12 and was discussed in Chapter 2. However, I have shown the alternative code in comments.

```
public class Text(string content) : IDocumentComponent
{
    private readonly string _content = content;

    public void Render(IRenderer renderer)
    {
        renderer.RenderText(_content);
    }
}

public class Section(string title) : IDocumentComponent
{
    private readonly string _title = title;
    // private readonly List<IDocumentComponent> _children = new();
    // Simplified form
    private readonly List<IDocumentComponent> _children = [];
```

```
    public void Add(IDocumentComponent component)
        => _children.Add(component);

    public void Render(IRenderer renderer)
    {
        renderer.RenderText($"-- {_title} --");
        foreach (var child in _children)
            child.Render(renderer);
    }
}
```

Implementing the Bridge Contracts (Renderers)

Let's implement the Bridge contracts now. This activity will help us see how different renderers produce output. Before you see the code, let me highlight a few points.

The two renderers will handle styles very differently, despite implementing the same IRenderer interface. This is the power of the **Bridge Pattern** in action:

- **The ConsoleRenderer (Immediate Action):** This implementation is **imperative**. The moment StartStyle is called, it changes the terminal's global state (its color). By calling the ResetColor() method, it resets the Console color to prevent style bleeding into subsequent output.

DESIGN NOTE

Why do we map styles to colors? The console does not support rich text formatting (e.g., bold or italic) in a standard way. In this example, I simulate these styles using different colors for demonstration purposes.

- **The HtmlRenderer (Stateful Buffering):** This implementation is **declarative**. It doesn't print anything during StartStyle; instead, it flips an internal switch (a boolean). It waits until RenderText is called to decide exactly how to "wrap" the text in HTML tags.

KEY TAKEAWAY

The Bridge pattern separates abstraction from implementation, allowing multiple rendering strategies to coexist under a common interface. While the abstraction defines the contract, each implementation is free to manage its own internal state and rendering strategy. The ConsoleRenderer and HtmlRenderer are intentionally designed to demonstrate this flexibility in practice.

It's time to explore the code. Let's begin with ConsoleRenderer:

```
public class ConsoleRenderer : IRenderer
{
   public void StartStyle(TextStyle style)
   {
      if (style == TextStyle.Bold)
         ForegroundColor = ConsoleColor.DarkBlue; // simulating bold
      if (style == TextStyle.Italic)
         ForegroundColor = ConsoleColor.Green; // simulating italic
   }
   public void EndStyle(TextStyle style)
   {
      ResetColor();
   }
   public void RenderText(string text) => WriteLine(text);
}
```

Author's Note: In the ConsoleRenderer, the last applied style will always win because each style directly sets the Console color. In other words, the Console maintains a single global color state, meaning each style change overwrites the previous one rather than combining with it.

REMINDER

The ResetColor() is a built-in method that sets the foreground and background console colors to their defaults.

You already saw that the abstraction and implementation can evolve independently. **As a result, style handling does not need to be identical across renderers. This is why, although the ConsoleRenderer does not combine styles, the HtmlRenderer can combine multiple styles by wrapping the text with multiple HTML tags.**

DESIGN NOTE

In this example, the HTML output is written to the Console for simplicity. In a real-world application, we could extend this design to write the output to a file, a web response, or another destination without changing the document structure. In addition, when multiple styles are applied, the HtmlRenderer wraps the text with nested HTML tags. Although the nesting order depends on the sequence of style application, in this simplified example, the visual result remains effectively the same.

Let's see the code now:

```
public class HtmlRenderer : IRenderer
{
    private bool _isBold = false;
    private bool _isItalic = false;

    public void StartStyle(TextStyle style)
    {
        if (style == TextStyle.Bold)
            _isBold = true;

        if (style == TextStyle.Italic)
            _isItalic = true;
    }

    public void EndStyle(TextStyle style)
    {
        if (style == TextStyle.Bold)
            _isBold = false;

        if (style == TextStyle.Italic)
            _isItalic = false;
    }
```

```
    public void RenderText(string text)
    {
        string result = text;

        if (_isItalic)
            result = $"<i>{result}</i>";
        if (_isBold)
            result = $"<b>{result}</b>";

        WriteLine($"<p>{result}</p>");
    }
}
```

DESIGN NOTE

In this implementation, the HtmlRenderer uses boolean flags to track whether a style is active. This means the current code is designed to handle **one level of nesting** per style type. While the Decorator pattern allows you to wrap components indefinitely (e.g., applying Bold multiple times), our simplified Bridge implementation would "turn off" the bold style as soon as the first EndStyle call is reached. For a production-grade system, you would simply replace these booleans with a **counter** or a **stack** to track multiple levels of nesting.

Adding Behavior Layers

Since we have implemented the core contracts, our foundation is built. Now, we can add "smart" features. Let's add styling and performance optimization without cluttering our original Text and Section classes.

Adding Style on the Fly Using Decorator

The following code uses the concept of the Decorator pattern. Here are the important characteristics:

- The DocumentDecorator is an abstract class that allows us to "wrap" any component. Two concrete classes, BoldDecorator and ItalicDecorator, inherit from it.

- The BoldDecorator doesn't change the component's text; it simply tells the renderer to "sandwich" the component's rendering between StartStyle and EndStyle calls.
- The other one—ItalicDecorator—follows the same approach.

Here is the code:

```
#region Decorator pattern

 public abstract class DocumentDecorator(IDocumentComponent component)
    : IDocumentComponent
{
    protected readonly IDocumentComponent _component = component;

    public virtual void Render(IRenderer renderer)
    {
        _component.Render(renderer);
    }
}

public class BoldDecorator(IDocumentComponent component)
    : DocumentDecorator(component)
{
    public override void Render(IRenderer renderer)
    {
        renderer.StartStyle(TextStyle.Bold);
        base.Render(renderer);
        renderer.EndStyle(TextStyle.Bold);
    }
}

public class ItalicDecorator(IDocumentComponent component)
    : DocumentDecorator(component)
{
    public override void Render(IRenderer renderer)
    {
        renderer.StartStyle(TextStyle.Italic);
        base.Render(renderer);
```

```
        renderer.EndStyle(TextStyle.Italic);
    }
}
#endregion
```

Smart Loading Using Proxy

The LazySectionProxy is used for performance optimization. It stands in for a real Section. Because it implements the same IDocumentComponent interface, the rest of our system doesn't know it's a proxy until the Render(...) method is called, at which point the real data is loaded.

```
#region Proxy pattern
// ===================== PROXY =====================
public class LazySectionProxy(string title) : IDocumentComponent
{
    private Section? _realSection;
    private readonly string _title = title;
    private void Load()
    {
        // If this section has not been created yet, create it
        if (_realSection == null)
        {
            _realSection = new Section(_title);
            _realSection.Add(new Text("Large document content loaded on demand."));
        }
    }
    public void Render(IRenderer renderer)
    {
        Load();
        // The following line would silently skip rendering if _realSection is null
        //_realSection?.Render(renderer);

        // Using the null-forgiving operator is safe here.
        // It is because Load() ensures _realSection is initialized
        _realSection!.Render(renderer);
```

```
    }
}
#endregion
```

DESIGN NOTES

In this example, each LazySectionProxy instance manages its own Section. Although the object is created only once, it is not implemented as a Singleton because different proxies may represent different sections with different data. The goal here is lazy initialization (Virtual Proxy), not global instance sharing.

In addition, as shown in the comment, the null-forgiving operator (!) is used in the Render(...) method because the Load() method guarantees that the real Section is initialized before use. Another approach would be to use the null-conditional operator (?.). However, this would silently skip rendering when the object is null, which is not desirable in this design.

Bridging the Past

We do not always build the entire system from scratch. Often, we must integrate "legacy" code—tools that are well-tested but don't match our new interfaces.

Let's assume that in our case, we have **a legacy printer that only knows how to print reports, but it does not support any formatting**. For simplicity, let's assume the following code:

```
public class LegacyPrinter
{
    public void PrintLine(string msg)
    {
        WriteLine("LEGACY: " + msg);
    }
}
```

How can we integrate it with our system? Once again, understanding design patterns can help you choose a suitable approach. Keep reading.

Using Adapter

Instead of rewriting the legacy tool (which might be risky or impossible), we can use the **Adapter** pattern. Let's see it.

In the following code, the LegacyPrinterAdapter acts as a "plug converter." It implements our modern IRenderer interface but delegates the work internally to the LegacyPrinter. As a result, the rest of the system can treat this legacy tool just like a modern renderer.

POINT TO NOTE

Since the legacy printer does not support styling, the StartStyle and EndStyle methods are intentionally left empty.

```
#region Adapter pattern
public class LegacyPrinterAdapter : IRenderer
{
   private readonly LegacyPrinter _printer = new();

   public void StartStyle(TextStyle style)
   {
      // No formatting supported
   }
   public void EndStyle(TextStyle style)
   {
      // No formatting supported
   }

   public void RenderText(string text)
   {
      _printer.PrintLine(text);
   }
}
#endregion
```

Author's Note: In this implementation, the adapter internally maintains a LegacyPrinter instance and delegates calls to it. Therefore, it is an object adapter. In C#, object adapters are more common than class adapters because the language does not support multiple inheritance of classes.

Orchestrating the Code

At this point, our system is complete. It is indeed powerful, but also complex. Why? Ideally, a client who wants to build a sample report should not have to manually instantiate sections, wrap them in decorators, and manage proxies. How can we simplify the system for the client? You guessed it right! It's time to implement the Facade pattern. Let's see it now.

Using Facade

The Facade pattern provides a high-level, simplified entry point to our sophisticated engine. Internally, it constructs the report using the logical structure shown in Figure 7-1.

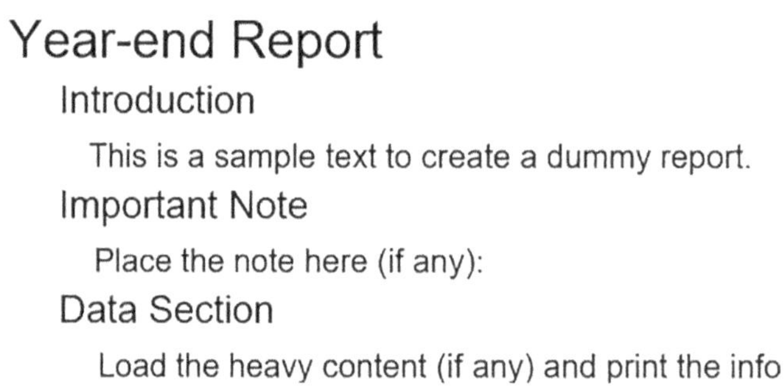

***Figure 7-1.** The logical structure of the report*

Let's see the code now:

```
#region Facade pattern

public class ReportFacade
{
    public static IDocumentComponent BuildSampleReport(
        string introText,
        int styleOption)
```

```
{
    var root = new Section("Year-end Report");

    var intro = new Section("Introduction");
    intro.Add(new Text(introText));
    root.Add(intro);

    var impNote = new Section("Important Note");
    var impNoteText = new Text("Place the note here (if any): ");
    if (styleOption == 1)
    {
        impNote.Add(new BoldDecorator(impNoteText));
    }
    else if (styleOption == 2)
    {
        impNote.Add(new ItalicDecorator(impNoteText));
    }
    else
    {
        impNote.Add(
            new BoldDecorator(
                new ItalicDecorator(impNoteText)));
    }
    root.Add(impNote);

    var lazySection = new LazySectionProxy("Data Section");
    root.Add(lazySection);

    return root;
}
public static void Generate(
    IRenderer renderer,
    string introText,
    int styleOption)
```

```
    {
        var report = BuildSampleReport(introText, styleOption);
        report.Render(renderer);
    }
}
#endregion
```

What happened here? The ReportFacade hides the internal "wiring." The client doesn't need to know how many patterns are working under the hood; they simply provide the data and a style choice, and the Facade orchestrates the Composite, Decorator, and Proxy patterns to produce the final result.

DESIGN NOTE

The ReportFacade provides a simplified entry point for constructing and generating reports. It orchestrates composite structure creation, decorator-based styling decisions, and proxy-based lazy loading integration. However, it does **not control rendering strategy selection**, which is delegated to the client via the IRenderer interface. This separation ensures that the document structure remains independent of output format, and the rendering strategy remains pluggable at runtime. In short, the facade focuses on document composition, not rendering implementation.

Author's Note: This centralized construction also makes it easier to migrate to a Dependency Injection (DI) system later if the project grows. I have discussed DI in detail in my other book *Creational Design Patterns in C#*.[1] However, it is beyond the scope of our current discussion on structural integrity.

Class Diagram

Before you see the client code, let us see the class diagram shown in Figure 7-2 as well.

[1] https://link.springer.com/book/10.1007/979-8-8688-1567-6

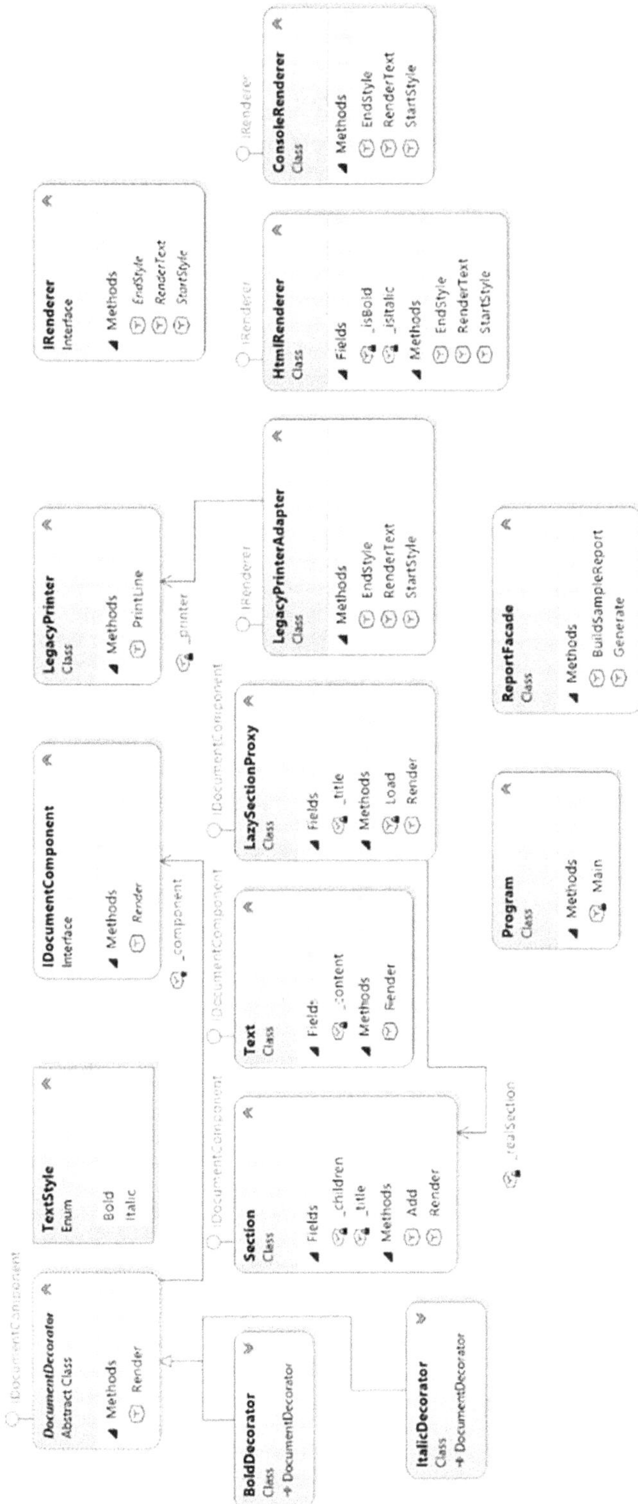

***Figure 7-2.** Class diagram of the report generation system*

The Client (Main)

Finally, we see how clean the Main method becomes. The client supplies the introductory text and only makes high-level decisions by choosing

- The rendering mode
- The preferred style

Here is a sample client:

```
#region Client code (Main)

class Program
{
    static void Main()
    {
        WriteLine("Choose rendering mode:");
        WriteLine("1. Console");
        WriteLine("2. HTML");
        WriteLine("3. Legacy");

        var choice =  ReadLine();

        IRenderer renderer = choice switch
        {
            "1" => new ConsoleRenderer(),
            "2" => new HtmlRenderer(),
            "3" => new LegacyPrinterAdapter(),
            _ => new ConsoleRenderer()
        };
        WriteLine("Enter introduction text: ");
        string input = ReadLine() ?? "Default introduction"; // For null-safety

        WriteLine("Choose style:");
        WriteLine("1. Bold");
        WriteLine("2. Italic");
        WriteLine("3. Bold + Italic");
```

```
            var styleInput = ReadLine();
            #region Using traditional switch statements
            int styleOption;
            switch (styleInput)
            {
                case "1":
                    styleOption = 1;
                    break;
                case "2":
                    styleOption = 2;
                    break;
                case "3":
                    styleOption = 3;
                    break;
                default:
                    styleOption = 1;
                    break;
            }
            #endregion

            // Passing the input now
            ReportFacade.Generate(renderer, input, styleOption);
        }
    }
}
    #endregion
```

DESIGN NOTE

I have used traditional switch statements in the client code. You can shorten the code by replacing it with the modern switch expression (introduced in C# 8) as follows:

```
#region Modern switch expression
int styleOption = styleInput switch
{
    "1" => 1,
```

```
        "2" => 2,
        "3" => 3,
        _ => 1
    };
    #endregion
```

Output

Let me show you some sample output now. You understand that these may vary depending on the selected option and supplied text.

Author's Note: While generating the outputs, I have kept the introductory text same in all cases: "**This is a sample text to create a dummy report.**" However, I have varied the remaining inputs that are shown in bold.

POINT TO NOTE

These cases highlight different aspects of the system—such as style composition (Decorator), rendering variation (Bridge), and legacy integration (Adapter).

Case-1

In this case, **HTML** rendering with **italic** style is chosen. The inputs and the corresponding output are shown here:

Choose rendering mode:
1. Console
2. HTML
3. Legacy
2
Enter introduction text: This is a sample text to create a dummy report.
Choose style:
1. Bold
2. Italic
3. Bold + Italic
2

```
<p>-- Year-end Report --</p>
<p>-- Introduction --</p>
<p>This is a sample text to create a dummy report.</p>
<p>-- Important Note --</p>
<p><i>Place the note here (if any): </i></p>
<p>-- Data Section --</p>
<p>Large document content loaded on demand.</p>
```

Case-2

This time, the same inputs as Case-1 are used, except that both **bold and italic** styles are chosen. Only the generated output is shown here for brevity (notice the change in bold):

```
<p>-- Year-end Report --</p>
<p>-- Introduction --</p>
<p>This is a sample text to create a dummy report.</p>
<p>-- Important Note --</p>
<p><b><i>Place the note here (if any): </i></b></p>
<p>-- Data Section --</p>
<p>Large document content loaded on demand.</p>
```

Case-3

In this case, **Console** rendering and **italic** style are chosen. The inputs and the corresponding output are shown here:

```
Choose rendering mode:
1. Console
2. HTML
3. Legacy
1
Enter introduction text: This is a sample text to create a dummy report.
Choose style:
1. Bold
2. Italic
3. Bold + Italic
2
```

-- Year-end Report --
-- Introduction --
This is a sample text to create a dummy report.
-- Important Note --
Place the note here (if any):
-- Data Section --
Large document content loaded on demand.

REMINDER

Since the Console does not support rich-text formatting (such as bold or italic) in a standard way, this example simulates these styles using different colors for demonstration purposes. Also, in our ConsoleRenderer, the last applied style always takes precedence because each style directly sets the Console color. Therefore, in the output, you will see the line "Place the note here (if any):" displayed in green. However, in the black-and-white paperback edition, the green color in the output will appear as black.

Case-4

In this case, **Legacy** rendering and **bold + italic style are chosen**. Only the generated output is shown here for brevity:

LEGACY: -- Year-end Report --
LEGACY: -- Introduction --
LEGACY: This is a sample text to create a dummy report.
LEGACY: -- Important Note --
LEGACY: Place the note here (if any):
LEGACY: -- Data Section --
LEGACY: Large document content loaded on demand.

Concluding Note

Before I finish, let me remind you that the current design can be extended further—for instance, by adding support for new output formats (such as PDF), additional styles, or more complex document elements like tables and images. I'd like to leave those exercises to you.

Summary

Congratulations! In **Part I** of this book, you learned six essential design patterns, and in **Part II**, you have built an application using that knowledge. Let's verify how these patterns interact with each other:

- **Composite**: Defines the hierarchical document structure
- **Bridge**: Decouples the document structure from rendering implementations
- **Decorator**: Adds styling behavior dynamically without modifying components
- **Proxy**: Enables lazy loading of expensive sections
- **Adapter**: Integrates legacy components into the modern system
- **Facade**: Simplifies client interaction by orchestrating the system

Without these patterns, the system would likely rely on conditional logic (for rendering types), tightly coupled classes, and direct modifications for new features. This would make the system harder to extend and maintain, especially as requirements grow.

In contrast, applying multiple patterns may increase the number of classes and abstractions. However, this trade-off allows the system to evolve with minimal impact on the existing codebase.

APPENDIX A

What's Next

This book covered six useful design patterns with many practical examples. Now, I encourage you to apply them in different projects, keep experimenting with new code, and continue learning. The reason is simple—practice makes perfect.

I also recommend exploring related topics through other books, articles, and blogs. However, do not overlook the classic GoF book listed below. Although it was published decades ago, its core principles remain highly relevant even in 2026. Modern programming languages indeed provide features that make certain patterns easier to implement. However, **design patterns themselves are not tied to any specific language.** Therefore, keep studying, practicing, and revisiting these ideas in your own projects.

I, too, keep experimenting with patterns and have written several books on design patterns using C# and Java. For example, ***Java Design Patterns 3rd Edition*** (Apress, 2022) and ***Design Patterns in C# Second Edition*** (Apress, 2020) covered all 23 GoF patterns and some additional patterns. These books also discuss anti-patterns and commonly asked questions on design patterns. One of my more recent books, ***Parallel Programming with C# and .NET***,[1] discusses Task-based Asynchronous Pattern (TAP) and related topics. If you are interested, you may find these resources useful as well. These books use different languages, but the underlying design principles remain the same.

In the following list, you will also find a few additional books from which I gained valuable insights during my exploration of design patterns. Although C# has evolved significantly and now includes many powerful features, I believe these books (or their updated editions) can still be highly effective learning resources.

[1] https://link.springer.com/book/10.1007/979-8-8688-0488-5

V. Sarcar, *The Structural Design Toolkit for C#*, https://doi.org/10.1007/979-8-8688-3029-7

Recommended Books

The following list contains my recommended books for you:

- *Design Patterns: Elements of Reusable Object-Oriented Software* by Erich Gamma et al. (Addison-Wesley, 1995)
- *Design Patterns in C#: A Hands-on Guide with Real-world Examples* by Vaskaran Sarcar, 2nd Edition (Apress, 2020)
- *Java Design Patterns* by Vaskaran Sarcar, 3rd Edition (Apress, 2022)
- *Head First Design Patterns* by Eric Freeman and Elisabeth Robson, Second Edition (O'Reilly, 2021)
- *C# Design Pattern Essentials* by Tony Bevis, First Edition (Ability First Limited, 2012)
- *Design Patterns For Dummies* by Steve Holzner (Wiley Publishing, Inc., 2006)

Additional Resources

In today's world, online platforms are very powerful. For example, you can learn from platforms such as Stack Overflow, Quora, YouTube, LinkedIn Learning, and Udemy, while search engines like Google can help you discover additional resources. These platforms can help you learn not only design patterns but almost anything you want. However, it is important to validate the content you consume.

In addition, throughout the chapters, I have referred to several links in the discussions and Q&A Sessions. You are encouraged to explore those links in detail to deepen your understanding.

Final Suggestion

As you continue exploring other patterns beyond this book, keep experimenting and think about trade-offs and OCP compliance, along with the practical usage scenarios to make your application flexible and maintainable. I wish you the best of luck!

Feedback and Support

Once you finish reading this book, I would request that you share your valuable feedback on the Amazon review page or any other platform you prefer. Any constructive feedback will help me improve future editions and write better books.

You also understand that any good quality work takes many days and many months (even years!). Many authors invest significant time and effort in producing quality technical content. You can encourage and help these authors by discouraging piracy. If you come across any illegal copies of our works in any form on the Internet, I would be grateful if you can directly report it to the Springer Nature Anti-Piracy Team.[2]

[2] https://www.springernature.com/gp/legal/piracy

APPENDIX B

Other Books by the Author

The following list includes Apress books written by the author:

- *Creational Design Patterns in Java* (Apress, 2026)
- *Delegates, Events, and Lambda Expressions in C#* (Apress, 2025)
- *Python Bootcamp* (Apress, 2025)
- *Creational Design Patterns in C#* (Apress, 2025)
- *Task Programming in C# and .NET* (Apress, 2025)
- *Parallel Programming with C# and .NET* (Apress, 2024)
- *Introducing Functional Programming Using C#* (Apress, 2023)
- *Simple and Efficient Programming in C#, Second Edition* (Apress, 2022)
- *Test Your Skills in C# Programming* (Apress, 2022)
- *Java Design Patterns, Third Edition* (Apress, 2022)
- *Simple and Efficient Programming in C#* (Apress, 2021)
- *Design Patterns in C#, Second Edition* (Apress, 2020)
- *Getting Started with Advanced C#* (Apress, 2020)
- *Interactive Object-Oriented Programming in Java, Second Edition* (Apress, 2019)
- *Java Design Patterns, Second Edition* (Apress, 2019)
- *Design Patterns in C#* (Apress, 2018)

V. Sarcar, *The Structural Design Toolkit for C#*, https://doi.org/10.1007/979-8-8688-3029-7

- *Interactive C#* (Apress, 2017)
- *Interactive Object-Oriented Programming in Java* (Apress, 2016)
- *Java Design Patterns* (Apress, 2016)

The following list includes the author's non-Apress books:

- *Python Bookcamp* (Amazon, 2021)
- *Operating System: Computer Science Interview Series* (CreateSpace, 2014)

To explore these books, you can visit any of the following links:

- https://amazon.com/author/vaskaran_sarcar
- https://link.springer.com/search?newsearch=true&query=vaskaran+sarcar&content-type=book&dateFrom=&dateTo=&sortBy=newestFirst

Index

V. Sarcar, *The Structural Design Toolkit for C#*, https://doi.org/10.1007/979-8-8688-3029-7

www.ingramcontent.com/pod-product-compliance
Lightning Source LLC
LaVergne TN
LVHW082336200926
848481LV00012B/3362
* 9 7 9 8 8 6 8 8 3 0 2 8 0 *